The Rehabilitation of the Alcohol Dependent

The New England Regional Rehabilitation Research Institute

Reuben J. Margolin, Project Director
George J. Goldin, Research Director

Northeastern University Studies in Rehabilitation

No. 8 *Social Disadvantagement and Dependency: A Community Approach for the Reduction of Dependency through Vocational Rehabilitation,* by George W. Craddock, Calvin E. Davis and Jeanne L. Moore, 1970.

No. 9 *Structure and Dynamics of Social Intervention: A Comparative Study of the Reduction of Dependency in Three Low-Income Housing Projects,* by Gary Spencer, 1970.

No. 10 *Psychodynamics and Enablement in the Rehabilitation of the Poverty-Bound Client: An Approach to Reducing Dependency,* by George J. Goldin, Reuben J. Margolin, Bernard A. Stotsky and Joseph N. Marci, 1970.

The Rehabilitation of the Alcohol Dependent

An Exploratory Study

Sally L. Perry
George J. Goldin
Bernard A. Stotsky
Reuben J. Margolin

Northeastern University Studies
in Rehabilitation Number 11

Heath Lexington Books
D. C. Heath and Company
Lexington, Massachusetts

Social and Rehabilitation Services of the
Department of Health, Education and Welfare reserves a royalty-free, nonexclusive
and irrevocable license to reproduce, pub-
lish, and translate or otherwise authorize
others to use this material, which was
developed out of Grant 12-P-55011/1-02.

This study is based upon investigation supported by Grant number 12-P-55011/1-02,
Social and Rehabilitation Services.

Printed in the United States of America

Library of Congress Number: 74-134014

Table of Contents

List of Tables

Preface

Dependence is a fact of life. Indeed, society demands mutual dependence for the enhancement of individual and group survival. Yet, when a person's dependency becomes overconcentrated on a particular individual, object, procedure, or system, it affects him adversely and is deleterious to the society of which he is a part. Thus, the community evidences concern when its members become overly dependent upon it and are unable to conform to the norms and values which govern the required level of self-reliance.

Overdependence upon people and the community is frowned upon because of its adverse social, economic, and psychological effects. There is yet another type of dependency, chemical dependency, whose adverse effects are physical as well. The steady increase of people's dependence upon drugs and alcohol to enable them to function is alarming. Not only is chemical dependency increasing, but the age of onset is now in many cases at the high school level and under. The individual, the family, and the community all pay a heavy price for such chemical dependency.

Alcohol dependency is of particular concern because alcohol is so readily accessible and addiction so insidious. Since a major part of the core research area of the New England Rehabilitation Research Institute is dependency, a study of the psychological and social factors in the lives of alcohol users, many of whom were almost totally dependent upon alcohol, was undertaken. The goal was to acquire information useful to the design of more successful techniques for the rehabilitation of the alcohol dependent and to explore the possibility of preventive rehabilitation.

In order to facilitate the reader's movement through this study, a brief summary of its organization is presented here. Following the introductory chapter, a comprehensive theoretical orientation is presented, summarizing what is known about the nature of alcohol use and the social and psychological factors thought to be associated with the etiology of alcohol dependency. The methodology involved in carrying out the investigation is described in some detail in the third chapter. Findings concerning the demographic characteristics of the research population and information obtained concerning drinking patterns, social and psychological factors in the alcohol dependent's family of orientation as well as findings concerning his marriage, his social skills, and the history of his vocational performance are presented and interpreted in the fourth through eighth chapters. Chapter 9 is a presentation of findings derived from psychological tests and behavioral measures. In the final chapter the findings of the study and their implications for implementation in the rehabilitation of the alcohol dependent are summarized.

Acknowledgements

We wish to express sincere appreciation to Mr. Neil Fallon, Regional Commissioner, Social and Rehabilitation Service, and his staff, for their consultation and enthusiastic support in bringing the research project upon which this volume is based to fruition. Our special thanks to Dean Martin Essigmann and his staff of the Office of Research Administration, Northeastern University. As always, we relied upon and received their wholehearted help.

Finally, we acknowledge with gratitude the cooperation and guidance of the following Salvation Army Staff Members:

Rev. George McCandlish
Counselor, Main Social Service Center
Salvation Army, Boston, Massachusetts

Major William Wilbur, Retired

Major Hugh C. Fleming
Boston City Welfare Coordinator
Salvation Army

Without the generous help and committment of these individuals, the study described in this book could not have been carried out.

1

The Alcohol Dependent and Rehabilitation

In the U.S. today estimates of dependence on alcohol[1] to function vary from a conservative 6,000,000 to an upper limit of 12,000,000; further, this figure is increasing at a substantial rate every year. The prevalence of alcohol dependency is probably even higher, since women are known to drink secretly in the home and often are not detected until they are in serious difficulty. In fact, the rehabilitation of the suburban alcohol dependent housewife is now recognized as a critical need. Because others in the alcohol dependent's life space are also affected, the social and emotional consequences to such persons and to society are incalculable.

The American public does not fully recognize the seriousness of the alcohol dependency problem existing in the nation at present. While most Americans express alarm at the increasing narcotics addiction, drinking is an accepted part of the culture. Even alcoholism is accepted with some degree of complacency. Yet, at this point in time, in size and in consequence to the well being of the nation, alcohol addiction is more serious a problem than narcotics addiction, since its harmful effects are more insidious and less dramatic.

The economic effects of alcohol dependency also loom as a serious problem. It is estimated that approximately 3 percent of the working force is affected by drinking to the detriment of industrial production. Thus, the nation has been referred to as suffering from a "billion-dollar hangover." When one considers the impact alcohol dependency has upon the nation in terms of impaired vocational, family, and community life, as well as its impact upon the crime and accident rates, the need for rehabilitation becomes strikingly evident. Reluctance of those addicted to deal with the problem directly (recognition) before it worsens complicates the problem.

---

[1]Since the definition of what is meant by the term alcoholic (alcoholism) is in such a state of confusion, the authors prefer to use the term alcohol dependent (alcohol dependency). No matter how one defines alcoholic, a dependency upon alcohol is a clearly visible phenomenon.

General Treatment Techniques, Rehabilitation Approaches, and Rehabilitation Facilities

This study was concerned not only with the treatment of the alcohol dependent but with his total rehabilitation. Rehabilitation is the process by which the individual suffering from alcohol involvement is helped to reduce his dependency upon alcohol so that he can raise his level of functioning in psychological, social, and vocational areas. Treatment of the symptom itself, in the conventional sense, is necessary but not sufficient to enable the individual to return to effective functioning on the job, in his family, and as part of the community.

During the past 50 years various treatment approaches have been attempted with varying degrees of success. Treatment techniques have essentially fallen into three categories: physiological (use of various drugs), psychological (use of various conditioning or negative reinforcement procedures), and psychotherapeutic. More sophisticated regimens for the treatment of alcohol dependency have utilized a combination of methods.

Rehabilitation facilities which serve the alcohol dependent are of two types: residential and nonresidential. Nonresidential facilities are located in various settings such as hospitals, alcoholic treatment centers, rehabilitation centers, community group work agencies, and psychiatric clinics. For the alcohol dependent unable to participate adequately in community rehabilitation, there are residential treatment centers such as hospitals, halfway houses, and correctional institutions which provide him with a sheltered setting. The halfway house does not necessarily offer a total residential experience since the alcohol user can leave the house to work.

Within these rehabilitation settings various processes are utilized. Techniques of conditioned negative response to alcohol (the association of unpleasant physiological states with drinking) and of chemotherapy, while initially successful, are not always permanent and do not deal with the underlying personality problems that may have led to the individual's drinking pathology. However, these techniques may be valuable when used in conjunction with counseling or therapy. Processes dealing with underlying personality problems include individual counseling, group counseling or therapy, physical and work therapy, vocational counseling, training and placement, vocational follow-up, and family casework where necessary. The range and level of rehabilitation procedures varies within and between settings depending on available facilities and the needs of the individual. Some rehabilitation agencies are specialized in terms of techniques relied upon to achieve the alcohol dependent's rehabilitation. For example, the state rehabilitation agencies base their approach upon rehabilitation counseling, while sheltered workshops direct their major commitment to a work adjustment process.

Quite different in structure from residential and nonresidential rehabilitation facilities are the affiliation type of organizations in which the alcohol dependent individual is motivated to seek a higher level of functioning through mutual support from other individuals having similar problems. An example of this type of organization is the "AA." Alcoholics Anonymous, a program which is psychother-apeutic in nature, has met with varying degrees of success with some alcohol dependents. The AA program relies heavily upon the principle of supportive group therapy plus the support of an informal individual counseling relationship. Rehabilitation has experimented with a number of diversified programs for the alcohol dependent. Just as some experts advocate short-term rehabilitation programs, others posit long-term programs in which physicians and other members of helping professions function in supportive roles.

One rehabilitation facility which has met with some encouraging success has been the halfway house. Most halfway houses have certain factors in common.

1. They are generally small in size, which fosters rapport, care, and identity for the client.
2. They are simple, informal, and unbureaucratic, with a minimum of rules.
3. They reduce status differences. Most halfway houses employ some recovered alcohol dependents as staff counselors. Even when staff are nonalcohol dependents, every effort is bent toward reducing status symbols that impede communication.

The halfway house is essentially a transitional experience between treatment setting and community living and relies on mutual psychosocial support by the residential group. Such nonresidential settings allow for what Fox and Lower (1968) called "daily testing in responsibility" which cannot be properly developed in a 24-hour residential program.

A similar type of resource being utilized is the comprehensive rehabilitation program housed and coordinated from a specialized rehabilitation center geared specifically for the rehabilitation of alcohol dependents. This type of center was used by the rehabilitation project at the Men's Social Service Center of the Salvation Army in San Francisco (Katz, 1966). A broad range of treatment techniques was involved, the use of which was based on the particular needs of the individual as well as on community resources such as the Division of Vocational Rehabilitation, the free adult education program, Alcoholics Anonymous, Al-Anon, and Al-Ateen. The men, who were homeless, lived at the centers and participated in the work program of the Salvation Army.

As determined by follow-up procedures, the reported success for those who remained in the project beyond the first three months and who received five or more sessions of vocational counseling was encouraging. Criteria of success were based upon measures of employment, sobriety, and social functioning. These outcomes, in turn, were related to such variables as length of stay in the project, type of therapy received, the extent to which vocational counseling was utilized, Alcoholics Anonymous involvement, and differential effectiveness of the program as a function of prior personal and social adjustment.

Another example of cooperation with a state Division of Vocational Rehabilitation in an effort toward the rehabilitation of the chronic alcohol dependent was a study conducted by the State of Florida Alcoholic Rehabilitation Program and Inpatient Center in Avon Park (Williams, 1964; Williams, 1967). Like the San Francisco project, success was measured by vocational adjustment, reduction of drinkng, and general social adjustment factors. Unlike the San Francisco project, the clients who participated evidenced a greater number of characteristics associated with middle class status.

Vocational rehabilitation counseling was the major rehabilitation treatment employed in this project. Comparisons were made between three groups: those referred for vocational rehabilitation services who were closed as unsuccessful, those who were closed as successful, and those who were not referred for vocational rehabilitation services (did not apply for such services). Again, the extent to which the services of vocational rehabilitation were used was regarded as of primary importance in the initial and sustained rehabilitation of the alcohol dependent.

Whatever rehabilitation treatment approach is utilized, it should be flexible, tailored to the individual needs of the patient, and reflect both the opinion of the rehabilitation professional as well as the preference of the patient. As Pattison (1966) pointed out, the low success rates reported for rehabilitating the alcohol dependent often reflect inadequate matching of the client to the treatment approach, not the intrinsic value of the treatment approach itself. Personality assessment prior to choosing a rehabilitation program can be helpful. (Partington and Johnson, 1969; Canter, 1966). It is obvious that chances of success are increased when the patient is allowed to help choose the course of treatment which he feels best meets his needs; in addition, such involvement in the rehabilitation program can provide him with a sense of self-determination.

Limited success in the rehabilitation of individuals dependent upon alcohol may be also related to the motivational level of the individual and to forces in the different social systems that infringe upon his life (family, etc.). Motivation is a constant problem in the rehabilitation of the alcohol dependent. Various social institutions have been utilized as motivators. The use of a helping authority such as probation, the courts, and law enforcement agencies has met with some success by making treatment and rehabilitation mandatory.

Nevertheless, basic to any rehabilitation program is the counseling process. For the alcohol dependent, counseling is of vital importance because his capacity to cope with the normative or conventional demands of society is impaired, tenuous, and in some cases totally absent. The usual psychotherapeutic methods have been tried with alcohol dependents and found wanting primarily because they rely to a considerable degree upon the ego strength of the client, his insight, and his capacity for self-determination. The confirmed alcohol user is grossly lacking in these strengths.

One claimed effective means of motivating the alcohol dependent for rehabilitation is based upon treating symptoms of alcohol dependence rather than analyzing personality factors which prove threatening to the client. Short-term treatment in which the sympton is replaced with imposed healthy behavior such as intense vocational and avocational activity has been found by some to achieve greater success than long-term conventional psychotherapeutic efforts.

Ego-oriented therapy has been favored by many professionals concerned with the rehabilitation of the alcohol dependent. In order to strengthen ego functioning and decrease ambivalence toward treatment, Ferneau (1968) advocated focusing primarily upon the area of conflict indicated by the presenting symptom. In the case of the alcohol dependent, the area of conflict would center around drinking behavior. By constantly relating other behaviors to the patient's dependence on alcohol, various conflicts or "ego-splits" (e.g., the patient's desire as an adult not to drink versus the patient's need as a child for oral gratification) could be resolved or integrated and a measure of insight achieved. He pointed to the superiority of this approach over that of the conventional psychotherapeutic approach in which the focus is on resolving underlying conflicts without due attention to the symtomatic behavior. Blum (1966) also pointed to the value of shifting emphasis from the resolution of childhood conflicts to the strengthening of ego functioning and enhancing the self-concept.

The importance of ego strength as a predictor of success in treatment was questioned by the efforts of Fowler et al. (1967). No relationship was found between scores on Barron's Ego-Strength scale, a measure of general personality integration, and the tendency of outpatient-clinic alcohol dependent males to remain in treatment (six or more interviews). Further, ego strength scores did not relate significantly to improvement in drinking behavior and other adjustment indices for those who remained in treatment for six months.

Similarly, White and Porter (1966) found that during the early months of sobriety self-concept and sobriety were negatively related. However, they postulated that their patients might have been experiencing advanced stages of what Dabrowski (1964) termed "positive disintegration" or a breaking down of the existing psychic structure prior to integration at a higher level of functioning. This concept appears similar to that of "regression in the service of the ego" which has been defined (Schafer, 1960) as a partial, temporary, controlled lowering of the level of psychic functioning to promote adaption. It promotes adaptation by maintaining, restoring, or improving inner balance and organization, interpersonal relations, and work." White and Porter suggested that a low self-concept may be characteristic of alcohol dependents for nearly a year after sobriety has been achieved. If the counselor involved in the rehabilitation of the alcohol dependent is not aware of such research he may initially become unnecessarily frustrated and discouraged by the seeming lack of client progress in the area of psychosocial adjustment; in turn, the client's motivation may suffer in response to the counselor's reaction.

Barriers to Rehabilitation

Several factors have been pointed out as major stumbling blocks to the rehabilitation of the alcohol dependent. The first critical factor has been the failure to bridge adequately the gap between the initial contact and subsequent treatment and rehabilitation efforts. In order to counteract the alcohol dependent's fear of the punitive and moralistic attitudes of the community which he has, over time, incorporated into his own self-image, a set of procedures must be devised in which a continuity-of-care concept has been built in and will be available throughout the entire rehabilitation process [see, e. g., Chafetz, 1968; Barton, 1968]. In other words, the structure of the program must involve integrated treatment efforts. Because the alcohol dependent has great feelings of unworthiness and consequently a need to be punished, he is both fearful and resistive to establishing relationships with others, especially persons affiliated with established community institutions. Thus, the psychosocial acceptance of the patient by staff is of paramount importance.

Munt (1960) suggested that resistence to treatment may be based on an intense fear of dependency. The alcohol dependent has discovered that alcohol can satisfactorily fulfill his dependency longings in a "safe" way. To project his needs from the bottle to another person might constitute a serious threat to the integration of his identity achieved with alcohol. Munt advocated immediate exploration of dependency feelings in order to minimize resistence to involvement in the conventional client- counselor relationship and to foster identification with the counselor for the working out of other problems.

On the other hand, Hershenson (1965) advocated work therapy preliminary to psychotherapy for alcohol dependents with weak identities. Work therapy might be less threatening to the patient and could function to better his self-image. Next, problems in interpersonal relationships could be dealt with; and, finally, with somewhat strengthened ego functioning, the patient could be confronted with and guided through areas of sensitive personal conflicts (e.g., dependency). Both approaches are valid, but choice of approach would depend on the individual client. Others have also dealt with the problem of dependency in the rehabilitation process (e.g., Lindt, 1959; Meyerson, 1953; Allen and Dootjes, 1968; Goldin and Perry, 1967).

Another obstacle to establishing a treatment relationship with alcohol dependents is their use of denial (Bell, 1965; Moore and Murphy, 1961). Denial of dependency on alcohol is the most prominent of the defense mechanisms employed by alcohol dependents and is an integral part of the alcohol dependency itself. Through drinking, the alcohol dependent is able to gratify his oral needs and achieve a sense of infantile omnipotence. This infantile omnipotence results in the alcohol dependent's fantasy that he can control his drinking. Moreover, he fears being labeled an alcoholic and fears the punitive and moralistic attitudes of society. His greatest fear, however, is the depression, experienced in the past when alcohol was temporarily unavailable to meet his dependency needs and in a future in which alcohol is denied him on a permanent basis. The importance of decreasing denial and increasing the alcohol dependent's acceptance of his problem is obvious in the establishment of a treatment relationship. Again, if too much emphasis is placed on underlying conflicts and not enough on the symptom itself (drinking behavior), the chance of decreasing denial behavior is likely to be less.

Another important obstacle to the rehabilitation of the alcohol dependent lies within the professional himself (Sterne and Pittman, 1965). Failure is often built into the rehabilitation process at the outset by the attitudes of staff toward the importance of motivation as critical to treatment success. If motivation is to be defined on the basis of current behavior, many alcohol dependents would be classified as unmotivated (i.e., denial of any need to be helped, fear of unmet dependency needs, difficulty in establishing interpersonal relationships, etc.). If a client is judged at the outset to be unmotivated and if motivation is considered crucial to recovery, it follows that the client will too often fail to meet the eligibility-for-treatment criteria.

Further, labeling a client already accepted for treatment as unmotivated because he fails to progress *like other clients* might suggest a certain rigidity in approach and in criteria of improvement. Relapses in sobriety should be expected to occur as they might in any chronic illness and not necessarily interpreted as lack of motivation or as justification for terminating treatment. Another inadequacy inherent in the concept of intrinsic motivation can be illustrated by the "highly motivated" alcohol dependent who presents himself for treatment during the withdrawal process. The health practitioner will quickly realize that this alcohol dependent does not desire help for his drinking problem but rather for the specific discomfort he is currently experiencing. Sterne and Pittman suggested that the concept of motivation be reexamined and that the helping professional learn not to use lack of motivation to rationalize his failure to rehabilitate the alcohol dependent.

Another aspect of the denial process is the alcohol dependent's unwillingness to accept his dependency on alcohol as his own doing. Androes et al. (1967) showed the effectiveness of employing Berne's "game" concept (from the book *The Games People Play*) as the basis of ward management. Whenever the alcohol dependent attempted to blame someone else for his drinking problem he was confronted with the role he was playing (alcoholic). His tendency to manipulate or maneuver others into the position of being the guilty or responsible party can be reduced within such a "game" framework.

Still another obstacle to successful rehabilitation is in the selection of goals for which the alcohol dependent is to strive. It has been suggested that, for some, total social, psychological, and vocational rehabilitation and total abstinence may be inappropriate and unrealistic (e.g., Brotman and Freedman, 1967; Pattison, 1966). Pattison stated that "abstinence may be maintained only at the expense of effective functioning in other areas." He demonstrated (Pattison et al., 1969) that improvement in the area of dependency on alcohol does not reflect in a linear fashion improvements in other adjustment areas such as the interpersonal, emotional, vocational, and physical. Further, Gerard, Saenger, and Wile (1962) noted that continued dependency on AA appeared to have resulted in poorer psychosocial adjustment for patients in their sample.

Blume and Sheppard (1967) had male alcohol dependents in a hospital rehabilitation unit rate themselves on various personality traits as sober and after a few drinks for the present and for 20 years ago. They found that alcohol compensated for certain personality deficiencies such as poor self-confidence, difficulty in expressing anger, and feelings of anxiety both early in life and at the time of the study; but that later in life the effects of alcohol were dysfunctional as well. Certainly, rehabilitation personnel should strive to achieve the maximal level of psychosocial functioning for their client; but they must also be aware that an optimal level does not necessarily require total independence from alcohol.

Although some encouraging strides have been made in the rehabilitation of the alcohol dependent, the total picture is far from optimistic. Much deeper knowledge of the socio- and psycho-dynamics of the alcohol dependent is required if effective rehabilitation programs are to be designed and implemented. The prevention of alcohol dependency must not be ignored. Changes in cultural attitudes, educational programs built upon understanding rather than guilt and fear, experimentation with early practical experience in the use and effects of alcohol, and early identification and treatment of potential alcohol dependents are among approaches that have frequently been suggested.

2 The Dynamics of Alcohol Dependency: A Theoretical Orientation

Regardless of the etiological premise(s) used in explaining alcohol-oriented behavior, dependency has been pointed out as an important contributing factor. As the pathology of the alcohol user progresses, he becomes increasingly dependent upon members of all social systems in which he participates. His family, his friends, and his coworkers all sooner or later become involved as targets of his dependent functioning. Finally, his financial dependency upon the community for support and, most important, his dependency upon alcohol itself cannot be ignored.

The definition of alcohol dependence is difficult. Some definitions are based on level of physical addiction. Others are based upon failure to adequately fulfill social and economic roles. There are also definitions which rely on psychological criteria. A definition by the World Health Organization (1952) describes alcoholics as:

Excessive drinkers whose dependence upon alcohol has attained such a degree that it results in noticeable mental disturbance, or in an interference with their bodily and mental health, their interpersonal relations, their smooth social and economic functioning, or those who show the prodromal signs of such developments.

A more sociologically oriented definition states:

Four facets of behavior set the alcoholic apart from his fellow drinkers. First, his use of alcohol regularly deviates from the typical drinking standards of his key social groups — home, neighborhood, and job. Second, the performance of his role in these key institutions is impaired. Third, he suffers from emotional and physical damage from his regular excessive use of alcohol. Finally, he shows an inability to stop drinking once he starts, even though he may know his drinking impairs his life; thus, his use of alcohol is beyond his conscious control. (Trice, 1966)

Although it is helpful to define alcohol dependence, definition is only a starting point. Some knowledge of the developmental aspects of alcohol dependence is necessary for those involved in rehabilitating the alcohol user.

Through the years, the etiology of alcohol dependence has been the concern of behavioral, biological, and physical scientists. Reported findings are far too voluminous to cite here, but what stands out in any literature survey is the lack of definitiveness concerning causality and the high level of disagreement concerning effective treatment and rehabilitation methods.

The current theoretical orientations to alcohol dependence may be summarized in the following statements.

1. Alcohol dependency may be characterized as a biopathology inherent in the body chemistry of the individual which, once triggered off by psychosocial events in his life space, sets up a physiological dependency on alcohol which follows a course of deterioration and organic disintegration in much the same manner as any other organic disease.
2. Alcohol dependency may arise intrapsychically. The alcohol dependent may have a particular psychological predisposition which develops as a result of interaction with family members during growth and development. Certain psychosocial events acting upon this predisposition trigger off a psychological dependence upon alcohol. The individual does not necessarily become physiologically dependent upon alcohol.
3. Alcohol dependency may be viewed as social in nature and conditioned by the norms and values of the given society. The alcohol addict is seen as an individual who cannot make the choices and decisions necessary to negotiate among the overlapping and conflicting standards set by society governing the use of alcohol.
4. Some consider the problem as involving all three causal systems. In other words, the alcohol dependent is defined as an individual with an organic potential for dependency upon alcohol coupled with a particular psychodynamic personality structure who is unable to cope with particular social and emotional demands in his milieu and deal with society's conflicting standards regarding alcohol use.

A survey of literature indicated that four major schools of thought have made the principle theoretical contributions to understanding the individual who becomes dependent upon alcohol. These are psychoanalytic, sociological, physiological, and learning theory.

Psychoanalytic Theory

The etiology of alcohol dependency suggested by the psychodynamic theorist is based upon the frustration, lack of fulfillment, or

overgratification of specific needs during the psychosexual development of the individual. Most psychodynamic formulations assume
that the person proceeds through specific stages of development
during which his relationship to the world about him is determined
to a major extent by the fixation or attachment of his psychic energy
(libido) to certain parts of his body and particular physiological or
bodily processes.

Thus, during the first year of his life (the oral stage), the infant's
primary satisfaction and major contact with the world is via his
mouth (sucking, biting, food taking, and spitting). During the anal
stage, encompassed by the second and third year, the child's major
gratifications and concerns are with sphincter control, toilet training,
and mastery of basic tasks requiring some muscular control. At
approximately three and one-half years of age early genital sexuality
begins to develop as the child's major concern and erogenous feeling
is transferred to the genitalia with concommitant sexual attachment
to the parent of the opposite sex, as well as rivalry with the parent of
the same sex. There is accompanying fear of bodily harm by the
parent of the same sex which the child resolves through identification with that parent.

During approximately six to ten years of age the child enters into
what is known as the latency period during which heterosexual
impulses are sublimated through educational and other achievements.
Cultural influences emphasizing sexuality seem to have shortened
this period considerably. At the onset of sexual maturity the child
enters into adolescence during which, for a brief period, there is
some reactivation of the Oedipal conflict (attachment to parent of
opposite sex) and some homosexual attachments. The time at which
actual adulthood is reached depends on the rate of psychosocial
maturation of the particular individual.

Early psychodynamic conceptualizations concerning alcohol dependency relied principally on the idea of deprivation or frustration
of the satisfaction of oral needs for love and nurturance or the
indulgence of these needs during the oral stage of psychosexual
development. Alcohol or the bottle was seen as an infantile
regression by which oral comfort was sought. More recent psychodynamic thinking on the subject of alcohol use proposes a more
complex interaction of dynamic forces.

Over 30 years ago Knight (1937) suggested that alcohol is used by
the individual as a means of coping with guilt over unconscious
hostility resulting from the environment's failure to gratify and
indulge his infantile demands. Knight described the alcohol dependent's family dynamics as involving a severe, dominating father

and an overprotective, indulgent mother. He classified alcohol addicts either as essential or reactive. In the essential type the person has poorly developed ego strength and mobilizes little anxiety over his failure to internalize norms and values. His capacity for forming meaningful interpersonal relationships is seriously impaired. The reactive alcohol dependent, on the other hand, although considerably more related to the norms and values of society, responds to its pressures and demands with dependency upon alcohol as a tension-reducing mechanism. Identifiable precipitating factors are generally absent in cases of the essential type; environmental stress was viewed as the precipitating factor in cases of the reactive type.

Fenichel (1945) described the alcohol dependent as an oral personality who depends upon alcohol to deal with internal inhibitions as well as external frustrations. Rado (1933) took the position that the alcohol dependent needed to regress to a state of high oral gratification. However, he attributed this need to anxiety over the individual's failure to develop an adequate self concept or identity because of poor opportunities for social experience and achievement. Higgins (1953) similarly proposed alcohol use as a defense against the individual's anxiety but did not feel that the anxiety necessarily stemmed from defects in psychosexual development at the oral stage. It was suggested that over a period of time the oral pleasure derived from drinking supersedes the value of alcohol as a means of resolving the original conflict.

Like Knight, Navratil (1959) viewed the overindulgent mother as a psychodynamic factor in the development of alcohol dependence. However, he highlighted the individual's conflict over his masculinity as a crucial factor. This conflict was seen as originating from the male's identification with a strong controlling, overindulgent mother and a failure to form an adequate identification with his father. Defects in identity formation during the anal (autonomy development) and phallic (genital sexuality development) stages have also been cited as associated with alcohol dependency. In other words, individuals are said to drink in order to cope with feelings of inadequacy which occurred during early psychosexual development.

Button (1956) described the difficulty encountered by the alcohol user whose failure to identify properly with the absent or feared father or with the dominant rigid father results in alternating needs to be masculine and "passive dependent" (homosexual). The hostility resulting from this conflict is said to manifest itself both externally and internally as self-destruction through the use of alcohol. Button also described the defenses and the breakdown of these defenses which the alcohol dependent mobilizes to cope with his anxiety and guilt over this conflict. However, he pointed out that similar personality dynamics exist in individuals who do not choose alcohol-involved behavior as a means of resolving the conflict.

Liansky (1960) questioned the total importance of the impact of early oral development upon later adult behavior as well as the significance of specific father-mother personality patterns, although the effect of parental ambivalence or inconsistency was acknowledged to be related to later psychopathology. Inadequate ego development was stressed as resulting from an imbalance of deprivation and overindulgence in early life which, in turn, predisposes the individual toward a strong need for dependency in adulthood. Further, the defenses such a dependent person are inadequate to resolve successfully the dependency-independency conflict encountered in some degree by all individuals. His use of alcohol to handle the conflict appears to succeed for a time, but, as the alcohol process develops, a "surrender to dependency" occurs and the once-repressed latent conflict over object ambivalences comes to the fore. Liansky used the term "regression" to refer to the restoration of observable ambivalences in interpersonal relationships such as the adolescent-like seeking out of male companionship, the unresolved Oedipal problems, and the drinking bout as a symbolic acting out of oral and homosexual impulses.

Chodorkoff (1964), like Liansky, pointed to inadequate ego development as characteristic of alcohol dependents and the use of alcohol as a means of compensating for ego deficiencies. Specifically, he dealt with ego deficiency as a result of early object loss or inadequate socialization by which the need for the means of establishing object relationships are motivated, learned, and conditioned. Through the use of alcohol and with the concomitant physiological bodily changes the individual is able to establish a primitive undifferentiated relationship with his own body as an object both available and safe. However, this relationship comes under constant threat during periods of sobriety. In order to alleviate the anxiety over loss of ego, the individual resorts again and again to the state of unconsciousness or stupor where the ego-body relationship is a solid, secure, and reassuring one.

Chafetz, et al. (1962) restated the lack of existence of any personality constellation unique to the alcohol dependent person.

Emotional traumatic deprivation experienced during the oral stage and an inadequate mother-child relationship was said to contribute to the alcohol dependent personality, but the severity of the problem is reflected by the level of psychosexual development attained. Because the use of alcohol gratifies directly and without anxiety, alcohol dependence was viewed as an oral perversion rather than a neurotic defense mechanism.

Through a variety of methodologies involving a variety of groups of alcohol dependents from a variety of settings, investigators have attempted over the years to determine whether common psychological characteristics or traits occur within the personality structure of alcohol dependents which would differentiate them from non-alcohol dependent persons. Most researchers have concluded that alcohol dependency does not involve a unitary personality configuration. However, a significant proportion of the studies does suggest the probability of common elements, although variable in relative strength and importance in the pyschic structure.

Alcohol dependents have generally been described in terms of the following: low frustration tolerance, prevalent anxiety; passive agression, dependency conflict; low self-esteem, low ego strength, poor self-concept, weak identity; narcissism, egocentricity, dependence, submissiveness, oral demanding; sexual immaturity, unconscious or latent homosexuality; blocked feeling expression, especially of anger and hostility; difficulty in the formation and maintenance of interpersonal relationships; self-debasement, self-punishment, self-hate; defensiveness, etc. As Fox (1965) pointed out, however, because nearly all research has used subjects already highly dependent on alcohol, the presenting behavior and personality traits might well reflect the effects of the addictive process, itself, i.e., regression to or fixation at an early level of psychosexual adjustment rather than the basic personality structure of the individual. In other words, what has been described as characteristic may be the *result* of alcohol dependency, not the *cause* of alcohol dependency.

Longitudinal studies, although without question the most difficult to undertake, may provide the most meaningful approach for determining etiology and providing appropriate preventative measures. The findings of two such studies (McCord, McCord and Gudeman 1959; Jones, 1968) indicated that the present personality characteristics of male alcohol dependents do, in fact, have their origins in adolescence or earlier *prior to* dependence on alcohol. Both studies pointed to the presence of an underlying intense independence-dependence conflict and an overemphasis on masculinity and independence in overt behavior. Subsequent dependency on alcohol provides one way of coping with (but not resolving) this conflict: an image of masculine adequacy is achieved by the public display of drinking like a man while at the same time the need for dependency is satisfied by drinking to intoxication. Desiring but denying the need to be dependent presents obvious problems in interpersonal relationships. Encouraging for those involved in the rehabilitation of the alcohol dependent, however, was the finding of Hurwitz and Lelos (1968) that a relatively small percentage of (occupationally stable) alcohol dependent males had actually incorporated into their self-concept their need for dependence. Prognosis is reportedly poorer for such individuals.

Sociological Theory

A sociological approach to the understanding of alcohol dependency is based primarily on the interaction between the individual and the normative and value structure within which he functions (Trice, 1956; Trice and Pittman, 1958; Pittman and Snyder, 1962; Markham, 1966; Reader, 1967). This approach involves the following "givens":

1. Based upon the early "Puritan Ethic" a great premium is placed upon the individual's maintenance of control over emotion and action. Since alcohol diminishes or eliminates such control, alcohol use which causes such loss of control is frowned upon.
2. In spite of the "Puritan Ethic" alcohol has come to be an accepted means to assist the individual in coping with the stresses, demands, and buffettings of our complex culture.
3. Although the American culture accepts the use of alcohol, its control over the individual's drinking is weak, inconsistent, and poorly defined. In other cultures use of alcohol is a completely accepted part of the learned life style (e.g., among French and Italians as a food and among Jews as a religious ceremonial vehicle). As an integral part of the culture drinking is by consensus governed through specific controls. In the American culture, however, there is a pronounced ambivalence relative to the use of alcohol. There is limited specificity regarding sanctions related to its use. Little is learned in the American family or community

which has any emotional strength in controlling drinking behavior. Since the American culture in its totality makes few provisions for specifying drinking behavior, it devolves upon the group within which the individual drinks to control drinking behavior.

The following statements describe the individual's attempts to adapt to the social givens stated above:

1. Drinking within a group setting provides the alcohol-prone personality with a number of rewards such as acceptance by and identification with an "in group," a superficial group relationship which is primary in psychosocial climate but requires none of the emotional demands of a primary or family group relationship, and the status which accrues with the ability to consume and hold quantities of liquor.
2. In the American culture each group within which the individual drinks establishes its own norms and values relative to tolerated drinking behavior. When an individual exceeds these norms, rather than control his drinking behavior as in other cultures, the group rejects the individual. Since the rewards of drinking-group membership are strong and the group sanction and control of the individual is weak, rejection by the group is gradual and not immediately perceived by the individual.
3. Rejection by the individual's drinking group exacerbates guilt feelings in regard to his loss of control (violation of "Puritan Ethic") and hence incurs his hostility toward the group. The individual is then faced with the choice of conforming to the group by exercising control of drinking in a situation where the group's control is undefined, or moving on to another group where fresh rewards will be forthcoming. First moves are horizontal to groups of similar social status. Subsequent moves are to groups of social status where the norms permit more excessive drinking behavior. After a series of group rejection-relocation experiences, the drinker finds himself in a state of social isolation.
4. Finally, the community reinforces the social isolation by labeling the individual as a drinker through such community processes as arrest, alcoholic treatment, etc. In this way the community structures the definition of the situation and forces the drinker's alienation from society's mainstream and into socially deviant groups.

Crabtree (1966) sought to identify through case studies some sociological and psychological factors common among alcohol dependents. Two such factors were high symptomatological anxiety and a high attitude ambivalence toward alcohol. Ambivalence was described as the result of exposure to conflicting parental behavior and attitudes toward the use of alcohol during childhood and/or exposure to group norms which conflicted with parental attitudes and behavior with respect to alcohol use. Partial confirmation of the hypothesis that both factors operate together to produce dependency on alcohol was obtained when groups of alcohol dependents and matched controls were compared.

Learning Theory

Dependency upon alcohol has generally been conceptualized within the framework of a reinforcement theory of learning (Dollard and Miller, 1950; Conger, 1956; Franks, 1958; Kepner, 1964; Kingham, 1958; Storm and Smart, 1965). Simply stated, reward or reinforcement, defined in terms of a reduction in drive state, is a necessary condition upon which an association between stimulus (alcohol) and response (drinking behavior) is learned. Assuming that a drive reduction principle is involved in dependence upon alcohol, the obvious question is what drive is being reduced. As Conger (1956) pointed out, the drive is rarely specified by learning theorists, although the strong oral and narcissistic needs postulated by the psychoanalysts are frequently commented upon. However, for the understanding of the acquisition of a strong stimulus-response association, one need not be aware of the specific drives involved. It is sufficient to consider the reduction through drinking of the manifest properties of the drive, such as anxiety or tension, even though the drive is obscurely tied to some specific source.

The initial association between the beverage alcohol and the drinking of it comes about in a number of ways. The individual may take his first drink to satisfy his curiosity or to be accepted by a group. However, the strengthening of the association must be accompanied by a reduction in the strength of a drive (pleasure or reduction of tension). In this manner, the response is rewarded, and in the presence of the same or similar stimulus conditions, the response is likely to be repeated.

Although many so-called "social" drinkers drink to reduce tension, their drinking behavior does not generalize to nontension situations. On the other hand, high dependency on alcohol results when drinking generalizes to many situations.

According to reinforcement theory, the process of alcohol dependency develops as follows:

1. Within the structure of some social or psychological situation the individual consumes an alcoholic beverage.
2. He may discover that the use of alcohol is rewarding (reduces anxiety, facilitates social relations, is pleasant tasting, etc.).
3. Because of the rewarding aspects of the response (drinking), when confronted with a similar stimulus in a similar situation, the individual is more likely to take a drink.
4. The probability of the individual's drinking increases with each pairing of stimulus and response.
5. If the individual's personality structure is such that alcohol reduces the tension and anxiety resulting from intrapsychic conflicts or other pain, then stimulus generalization may ensue; that is, the individual no longer drinks for the original reasons but begins to drink in other situations.
6. As the individual continues to drink, numerous other cues arising from the drinking situation (such as time of day, etc.) become associated with drinking and elicit this behavior.
7. The individual's response (drinking) is further strengthened by his need to avoid the pain (psychological as well as physical) of sobriety.
8. Finally, the need for the stimulus (alcohol) becomes so great (dependency) that other painful responses (hangover etc.) are overshadowed by the original pleasurable response. This is explained by the principle of the gradient of reinforcement in which immediate reinforcement more than compensates for delayed adverse effects.

At this point it is important to consider Dollard and Miller's model of approach-avoidance conflict behavior as it applies to alcohol use. It has been established that the closer one approaches an unpleasant goal, the greater the fear and conflict which motivates the avoidance of this goal. Alcohol is capable of reducing avoidance of the goal (unpleasant stressful situations) without changing the strength of approach to it. Therefore, the individual can use alcohol to reduce avoidance and thus enable himself to cope with stressful life situations, even though the coping process may be socially unacceptable.

Evidence supporting this theory has been accumulated using experimentally produced fear in animals as the drive. This would indicate that increasing motivation of approach behavior without decreasing avoidance only serves to raise the anxiety level of the individual. Thus, if we view the therapeutic implications of this theory, we are led to believe that no amount of motivation of the alcohol dependent to reduce drinking would be effective, unless the anxiety producing the avoidance behavior is dealt with and resolved.

In an interesting and unique fashion Storm and Smart (1965) applied some of the principles involved in learning theory toward the understanding of various aspects of alcoholic behavior. Predicated on previous animal research in which drugs were used, the authors suggested that responses learned under the influence of alcohol would not transfer to the sober state or vice versa. This is based upon a learned discrimination between the two states and a failure to generalize from one to the other. The differences between the two states (intoxicated and sober) involve the differences in the physiological state of the central nervous system (proprioceptive stimuli arising within the organism) which occur as a result of alcohol ingestion. Following from this is that the larger the amounts of alcohol consumed and the greater duration of time in which these amounts are consumed, the greater will be the generalization decrement (failure to generalize). When the generalization decrement is sufficiently great, it is referred to as dissociation.

The dissociation hypothesis can be used to explain the blackout and loss-of-control phenomena. In the case of the blackout (amnesia), the dissociation between the intoxicated and sober states is complete and none of the behavior while drunk is remembered by the individual at sobriety. Simply stated, there is no transfer of learning. The authors suggest that after experiencing a blackout recall, insight, etc. may only be possible by reproducing the alcoholic state. In the case of less complete dissociation, memory is retained but transfer of responses is essentially limited. For example, an individual under the influence of alcohol may to some extent reduce shyness and become more aggressive, outgoing, and communicative. But this behavior does not transfer to the sober state. Similarly, socialized conformity responses learned by the individual under the sober state may not remain totally intact after he consumes several drinks.

In the case of loss of control as a result of drinking, the physiological changes associated with having one drink set up cues which trigger off the chain of responses associated with having another and another drink. In order to decrease the strength of this response or behavior, Storm and Smart suggested that the individual must learn to respond to the cues of increasing intoxication by not drinking in the intoxicated state. In other words, the learning of such behavior in a sober state is irrelevant (lack of transfer); the unlearning of one response and its replacement with another must occur under the stimulus conditions (physiological state) under which the response was originally learned.

This theory suggests implications for therapy and research. Namely, individuals can be helped to respond to alcohol-associated cues in a different manner so that excessive drinking habits can be unlearned and replaced by controlled social drinking. This idea is contrary to current therapeutic practice, but low success rates in treating and rehabilitating alcohol dependents impels us to suggest that this approach is worthy of further exploration.

Dependency on alcohol has been conceptualized in terms of conflict resolution (Heilizer, 1964; Wetherbee, 1966). The controlled drinker is described as one who holds a positive attitude toward alcohol and drinks according to a negative feedback system (approach-avoidance conflict model) in which the need to drink is reduced the more he drinks. In contrast, the uncontrolled drinker holds a negative attitude toward alcohol and drinks according to a positive feedback system (avoidance-approach conflict model) in which the need to drink is actually increase the more he drinks. For the controlled drinker, primary motivation to drink is in response to a stress situation in the external environment whereas drinking for the uncontrolled drinker is primarily motivated by a stressful feeling within himself.

Physiological Theory

Physiological orientations to the etiology of alcohol dependence are predicated on the supposition that certain persons are inherently vulnerable to the effects of alcohol. Generally, these theories point to chemical, metabolic, or endocrinological disorders or imbalances. Research has thus far failed to substantially demonstrate the link between such constitutional defects and susceptability to alcoholism. However, the possibility that future discovery will demonstrate the existence of physiological processes or abnormalities cannot be ignored. For example, the March 2, 1970 issue of Newsweek printed the following research note:

A good many physicians, psychiatrists and sociologists assume that the alcoholic suffers from a personality defect which forces him to seek oblivion in a bottle. But now, researchers at the Houston Veterans Administration Hospital have produced evidence that alcoholism may be a physical disorder. Indeed, their studies suggest that alcoholism may be very much the same as narcotic addiction.

The chain of evidence is complex, but Drs. Virginia Eischen Davis, Michael J. Walsh and Yasmuitsu Yamanaka believe the body may produce narcoticlike substances as a result of long-term use of alcohol. Their theory is based on chemical studies made of rat brain and liver tissues in the test tube. When alcohol is introduced into the test tube, it is converted into acetaldehyde. This substance, they found, inhibits the action of an enzyme called aldehyde dehydrogenase which is required for the normal breakdown of dopamine, a key chemical in the brain. Dopamine normally is converted into an acid derivative. But because of the impaired enzyme action caused by alcohol, dopamine becomes THP — a chemical from which the opium poppy creates morphine. The researchers think the alcoholic's body may also turn THP into addicting substances.

Since this study is concerned with the psychological and social aspects of the rehabilitation of the alcohol dependent, physiological or biochemical aspects of alcoholism will not be examined (for a review of these theories see Armstrong, 1959).

3 General Purpose, Goals, Methodology

In hopes of providing the rehabilitation practitioner with greater understanding of the socio- and psychodynamics of alcohol dependency, this research was organized to investigate the occurrence and possible developmental impact of certain life-history events in key areas of psychological and social functioning which might be related to the individual's subsequent development of dependency on alcohol. In addition, the current functioning ("here and now" factors) of the alcohol dependent subjects was examined using both test and behavioral measures. A review of the literature revealed no other study which involved such a tri-dimensional approach: biographical (social-historical), psychological, and behavioral.

In general, information concerning the psychological aspects of dependency in interpersonal relationships within the family and marital situations as well as data pertaining to social aspects of dependency in such areas as community affiliations, drinking behavior, vocational history, and antisocial behavior were obtained using the interview technique. In addition subjects rated their own need for dependency and conflict over dependency needs via self-report indices. Since discrepancies between self-concept and actual performance are not uncommon, laboratory-type behavioral measures were administered to tap situational dependency.

The major goal was to provide information in the following areas which might have applicability to the rehabilitation of the alcohol dependent:

1. The value of psychological and social structure in rehabilitation situations, both in counseling and in facilities (sheltered work shops, rehabilitation centers, etc.).
2. The value of psychological tests in early identification of dependency in alcohol dependent clients, both in terms of dependency level and conflict over the need to be dependent.
3. The understanding of particular events in the biography of the alcohol dependent which might have influenced his dependence upon alcohol, and the design of methods to deal with the results of these events in the rehabilitation process.
4. The development of rehabilitation techniques by which meaningful interpersonal relationships may be established to supplant dependence upon alcohol.

Rationale for a Skid-Row Sample

From a rehabilitation standpoint the skid-row alcohol dependent is not totally different from the nonskid-row alcohol user. The executive who drinks within the walnut confines of his office, the depressed housewife who drinks in the loneliness of her kitchen, and the homeless man who drinks huddled in some skid-row doorway have much in common. They are all dependent, dependent to varying degrees and within the framework of differing life space demands but, nevertheless, dependent. The rehabilitation techniques required to treat (i.e., reach, motivate, and involve) these dependent persons may differ in external approach, but all are undergirded by similar psychosocial principles.

The authors felt most could be learned about the rehabilitation of alcohol dependents by studying those totally dependent. For this reason a skid-row population of subjects was chosen for the study. The group of alcohol dependents who inhabit skid row is, by definition, dependent upon alcohol. Moreover the dependency of the alcohol user on skid row extends beyond the chemical dependency upon alcohol to almost total dependency upon the community as well.

Skid row is composed of many types of individuals, all of whom are poor. The alcohol dependent is but one of these types. He, like others, may be characterized as having a high rate of unemployment or irregular employment and incredibly low income. His presence on skid row involves a heavy cost to the taxpayer in terms of excessive dependency on social agencies, medical facilities, and the courts.

The alcohol dependent is on skid row because of his total rejection and isolation by the community coupled with his economic instability and inadequacy. He finds skid row a conducive life style, because the loosely structured normative system makes little in the way of demands upon him for conformity in such areas as employment, physical appearance, drinking, sexual behavior, etc.

The skid-row alcohol dependent has many "keepers" (objects for his dependent strivings). Police frequently protect him from being robbed or beaten, and from freezing to death. Social agencies, missions, and health agencies provide him with food, clothing, shelter, recreational facilities, medical attention, etc. Also, a unique labor market (short-term jobs) is available where payment is immediate to insure constant alcohol supply and to meet other current needs. Small loosely formed social "cliques" provide the alcohol dependent on skid row with some measure of protection and sharing of material possessions. In short, skid row provides the alcohol dependent with an encompassing milieu which satisfies his dependence, both psychological and material, in a total manner.

Early studies involving alcohol dependents focused primarily upon homeless men on skid row or chronic drunkenness offenders. These groups were the most easily identifiable and most accessible. Both groups, although not identical, evidenced a considerable lack of family and marital ties and relatively low vocational stability and skill. Undersocialization, i.e., minimal opportunity early in life to acquire adequate social and interpersonal skills, was believed to be an important contributing factor in alcohol dependence (Bacon, 1944; Straus, 1946; Straus & McCarthy, 1951; Pittman & Gordon, 1958). This could have led to the discovery that alcohol could compensate for deficiencies in interpersonal skills and serve as a vehicle by which feelings of group identity, membership, and acceptance could be achieved without the consequences of reciprocity. Skid row provides a subculture within which ends can be attained with a minimal use of social groups, demands made by others are negligible, and controls placed on behavior are essentially nonexistent.

Jackson & Connor (1953), focusing on independence-dependence conflict, pointed out the functionality of the skid-row subculture to the alcohol dependent. The alcohol dependent can deny his dependency needs through identification with the skid-row life style, thus enabling him to meet his need to maintain a self-image of independence (no controls on his actions, no responsibilities to meet). Furthermore, he can maintain a sense of masculinity through drinking behavior while simultaneously satisfying his need for dependence. Because the surfacing of the independence-dependence conflict is so threatening to the alcohol dependent, Jackson and Connor suggested that dealing with such conflict during the middle and later stages of therapy might be a more fruitful approach to rehabilitation.

An alternative to the *under*socialization hypothesis in explaining the relative detachment of skid-row alcohol dependents is the *de*socialization hypothesis (Rooney, 1961). Here it is postulated that social interaction skills have been lost or have deteriorated through disuse. In other words, social isolation is the result of alcohol dependence among homeless men rather than a contributing factor. The *under*socialization proponents would suggest socialization as a rehabilitation approach whereas the *de*socialization advocates would suggest the implementation of a *re*socialization program.

With the advent of studies dealing with clinic and hospital

populations, many of the stereotypical characteristics previously ascribed to alcohol dependents i.e., alcohol dependents marry to a significantly lesser degree than do "normals," etc. were dispelled. Furthermore, it was discovered that skid-row alcohol dependents constituted a small percentage of all alcohol dependents. In an attempt to deal with the concept of social isolation as it applied across groups, Singer et al. (1964) compared alcohol dependent patients (both emergency ward and medical/surgical admissions) with nonalcohol dependent patients. Although the emergency-ward patient evidenced greater social isloation (as measured in terms of current social contact, social stability, and voluntary use of social resources) than the medical/surgical admission, both alcohol dependent groups were more socially isolated than the nonalcohol dependent patient. The data, then, supported the hypothesis that alcohol dependency is at least *accompanied* by social isolation which is manifested more among skid-row men than among those displaying greater conformity to the norms and values of the larger society.

The process of socialization into the skid-row life style was analyzed by Bahr (1967). Support or partial support was found for hypothesized positive interrelationships among the variables — identification with skid row (skid row as "home"), interaction with other men on skid row, and conformity to skid-row drinking behavior. Interestingly, length of time on skid row proved to be an intervening variable. Those who had lived on skid row for ten years or more, those who had already been "socialized," did not display the continued need for social interaction to the extent that the "newcomers" did.

In another study of homeless Bowery residents, Bahr and Langfur (1967) found that *within* this socially detached subculture the currently "heavy" drinkers evidenced a greater degree of overall attachment both in terms of past and present organizational memberships in society (especially in areas of recreational, church, and familial affiliations) than did "moderate" drinkers or "abstainers." Rooney (1961) found that "winos" were motivated more by interactional than economic needs in their formation of bottle gangs. These studies suggest that social skills, although variable in quality and range of applicability, do exist and can serve as a basis for behavior modification, whether by means of socialization or resocialization.

Subjects

Fifty-five male alcohol dependents who frequented the Salvation Army's South End Corps in the skid-row section of Boston served as subjects. Choice of subjects was determined by willingness to participate and frequency of attendance at the center. Selection was made by the center's counseling staff. Nearly the total population was sampled, excluding those who were transient visitors and/or were judged to be intoxicated at the time of interviewing. The majority of the men were between the age of 45 and 65 and could, therefore, provide the experimenter with fairly comprehensive information regarding family, drinking, and vocational history.

Research Instruments

Psychodiagnostic Indices

Navran Dependence (Dy) Scale. The construction of the Dy Scale (Navran, 1954) was based upon the selection of items from the Minnesota Multiphasic Personality Inventory which, in the opinion of judges, measured dependency. Fifty-seven such items were chosen for the final true-false scale. This self-report test purports to measure the extent to which persons describe their own personality characteristics in terms of what the team of judges described as dependency. Since a person may be in conflict over his need for dependency on others (in part due to the emphasis placed by society on independent functioning) and thus deny that dependence, scores at *either* extreme of the scale may also be interpreted as indicating strong dependency needs.

Marlowe-Crowne Social Desirability Scale. The purpose of this self-report test (Crowne & Marlowe, 1964) is to assess the extent to which people describe themselves in a socially desirable way in order to obtain the approval of others. The scale consists of 33 true-false items. It was hoped that by administering the M-C Scale to the research sample something might be learned about the extent to which relatively unattached alcohol dependents relate to and endorse the cultural norms of the larger society.

The Predicament Story Test. Developed by Schwaab (1959), this multiple choice test serves to differentiate persons who are in conflict over their dependency needs from those who are not. Further, those who show conflict may be subsequently differentiated in terms of resolution of conflict. Eighteen situations are presented in which the hero of the story is confronted with a predicament; five alternative solutions are offered.

The "vacillator" is defined as one most often choosing no realistic solution. He is described as ambivalent, indecisive, and hesitant, feeling most secure by not acting at all. The "acceptor" is defined as one who most often allows someone or something external to himself determine his future. He is described as a passive-submissive person who obtains satisfaction through the independent behaviors of others. The "denier" is defined as one whose defense against his dependent needs takes the form of reaction formation. He is described as one who feigns initiative and appears to be terribly self-sufficient and sure of himself but, in reality, is not.

Minor modification in wording was introduced in order to make the test more appropriate for the subject group. For example, the occupation of professor was changed to machinist so that the subjects could more easily identify with the hero of the story. This test was not designed to measure dependency per se but rather possible existing conflict over dependency.

Behavioral Measures

Thematic Apperception Test (TAT). Two cards (6 BM and 20) were presented to the subject with the standard instructions to make up as dramatic a story as possible, giving circumstances which led up to the situation, what is happening at present, the feelings of the persons involved, and the outcome. The first card is described as follows: "a short elderly woman stands with her back turned to a tall young man. The latter is looking downward with a perplexed expression." The second card is described as: "The dimly illuminated figure of a man (or woman) in the dead of night leaning against a lamp post."

The response measure used was time to respond to the relatively *structured* stimulus situations. The purpose was to ascertain the relative ease or difficulty with which a person of a measured degree of characteristic dependency is able to react to a new stimulus situation of a relatively structured nature by defining it.

Rorschach. Two Rorschach cards (6 and 9) were presented to the subject with the standard instructions to report what is seen in the inkblot designs. Like the TAT, the response measure used was time to respond to the relatively *unstructured* stimulus situation. The verbal material was also recorded. Again, the purpose was to assess the relative ease or difficulty with which a person of a measured degree of characteristic dependency is able to react to a new stimulus situation of a relatively unstructured nature by defining it.

The Letter "M" Puzzle. This task consisted of an extremely difficult jigsaw-type puzzle composed of six wooden pieces. Subjects were not told what letter could be formed or how much time would be allowed; they were simply instructed that, if put together correctly, the pieces would form a letter of the alphabet. Ten minutes were allowed for the task. The experimenter recorded all responses made by the subject while he worked on the puzzle as well as the time of each response. The purpose was to determine the extent to which alcohol dependents would exhibit overt dependence on the experimenter in terms of help-seeking behavior in their efforts to solve the problem.

Number Judgment. The third decision-making task contained, in addition to the variable of structure, a form of risk or consequence resulting from the decision. The subject was presented two sets of fifty cards; each card of each set contained one of four numbers. The object of the game was to guess which of the four numbers would occur most frequently in the entire deck. The maximum number of cards that could be shown the subject was twenty-five. The two sets of cards varied in level of difficulty. The order of presentation was alternated so as to control for this variable.

In general, the subject was shown the first five cards and instructed that for every additional card he wished to see after the first five cards he would lose one cigarette out of a pack of twenty cigarettes. When the subject felt that he "knew" the answer, he would stop the experimenter and make known his guess. If he were wrong, he was told that he would receive no cigarettes; if correct, he would receive the remaining cigarettes. Cigarettes were felt to provide a meaningful reward to the skid-row alcohol dependent for two reasons: (1) observation indicated that cigarettes had an important "trade" value in the obtaining of liquor or wine and that smoking cigarette butts from the street or ashtrays was a common occurrence; (2) according to some theorists, alcohol dependents are essentially oral characters — cigarettes would provide another means of oral satisfaction.

For this task the amount of information (the number of cards, including the first five) required by the subject was the response measure used. The purpose was to ascertain the relative amount of information needed by the more or less dependent subject before he felt "secure" enough to make a decision in which a consequence of his choice would result.

Welsh Figure Preference. This task consisted of a sheet of eight equally divided sections, each containing a visual stimulus. The visual stimuli varied in structure from the highly structured geometric design to the completely abstract design. The subject was instructed to rank the eight figures in order of preference. The purpose was to assess the relative appeal of the figures to persons of various levels of characteristic dependency.

Drawing Completion Test. This task consisted of a sheet of paper equally divided into twelve parts; each part contained a combination of two or three straight or curved lines, some connected, some not. Given a pencil, the subject was simply instructed to do whatever he liked with the lines. A 5-point scale score was obtained for each subject on the basis of flexibility-rigidity of approach. A rigid approach might be characterized by the following: a simple connecting of lines, closing up figures, making many of the same type of figures (stereotype), etc. A more flexible approach would be characterized by the following: expanding the lines, creating a new "picture," etc.

Interview

Each subject was interviewed for the purpose of obtaining information concerning past and present drinking patterns, family history, marital history, vocational history, treatment patterns, demographic information, present modes of functioning, etc. The interviews required approximately one to two hours to complete and were relatively unstructured in nature.

Analysis of Data

All data pertaining to test and behavioral measures were punched directly on to IBM cards; biographical data were first categorized and coded and then punched on to IBM cards. Computer analysis was based upon the Data-Text System (a computer language for social science research) developed at Harvard University by Couch (1967).

The general scheme of analysis involved the following forms: (1) intercorrelations *within* the three areas of dependency measurement: test, behavioral, and biographical (social-historical); (2) relationships *between* the three areas of dependency measurement: test and behavioral, test and biographical, and behavioral and biographical. Statistical techniques employed were the Chi square test (or Fisher exact probability test, where appropriate), *t*-test, and one of variance. For a statistical value to be accepted as significant, the value had to have a probability of 5 percent or less. Trends were presented when they had supportive value for relationships found to be statistically significant.

A more detailed description of data analysis pertaining to test and behavioral measures is presented in Chapter 9. Chapters 4 through 8 deal exclusively with biographical measures and analysis is based entirely upon the nonparametric statistical tests described above.

4 Demographic and Social Characteristics of the Research Population

In any study it is important to construct a profile or picture of the sample studied on the basis of its demographic and social characteristics. Such a profile enables the reader to view subject performance in better perspective.

Seventy percent of the totally male population were between 45 and 64 years of age.[1] Forty-six of the men were of Caucasian origin; 8, black; and 1, American Indian. One-tenth never completed grammar school, and over half never completed high school. However, one-fifth obtained some education beyond the high school level. The educational level of the subjects' parents was slightly lower than that of the subjects for elementary and secondary grades, but one-fifth did continue their education beyond the high school level. Two-thirds of the subjects' fathers were employed at the skilled level or better; of the mothers who worked, one-half were employed at the skilled level or better.

At the time of the study over half the alcohol dependents were without an address. Frequency of appearance at the Salvation Army center was daily for approximately two-thirds. Although the center provided the alcohol dependent some measure of physical comfort (e.g., warmth, a place to nap, a pair of shoes, an overcoat, etc.) as well as an opportunity for social interaction, it also represented a link between the skid-row subculture and the larger community. The very fact that these men still had the remaining minimal ego-functioning to seek survival (Eros supercedes Thanatos) from a community resource is an encouraging sign. Eighteen percent of the men received some form of public assistance while 20 percent received financial assistance other than public assistance (social security, pensions, disability payments, etc.).

Chronic disability was reported by 23 of the men; for the majority the disability did not prevent employment, although type of work done may have been limited. Specifically, the following general physically handicapping conditions were reported: cardio-

---

[1]Because some men did not supply information or sufficient information pertaining to certain variables, percentages throughout the study are based on the number of men whose responses were adequate for coding rather than based on the number of men in the sample.

vascular (4), pulmonary (5), orthopedic-neuromuscular (9), and metabolic (1) disorders; epilepsy (2); and impaired hearing (2). Included are three subjects who reported both an orthopedic- and a nonorthopedic-neuromuscular condition but were categorized according to the latter disability.

The vast majority of men were not employed at the time of the interview; some of these reported occasional daily work once or twice a month at the maximum. The remaining men reported working regularly at "spot jobs" once a week or more. Nearly 60 percent had not held a regular full-time position for anywhere from one year to over twenty years and many had not even taken "spot" labor for six months or more.

Manpower and labor pools offer the men on skid row the most used source of employment. About half of the men claimed to still be actively seeking employment, while over a quarter reported themselves unable to work due to an acute or chronic disability. The majority stated that they desired full-time employment. For a detailed breakdown of descriptive data see Tables 1 through 4.

Some interesting relationships involving demographic variables were noted. Two such relationships were: subjects who at the time of the interview reported having a place to live also reported receiving financial assistance other than (not necessarily in addition to) public welfare. Moreover, these same men interacted minimally at the Salvation Army center, essentially keeping to themselves. On the other hand, those who reported having no room or place to sleep interacted moderately or extensively with the other men at the center. These relationships are presented in Tables 5 and 6.

These findings suggest that even in the culture of deprivation, of which the skid-row alcohol dependent is a part, there may be a status hierarchy based on socioeconomic factors. Thus, those subjects who lived a more secure life with a regular income felt little in common with those whom they perceived as lacking the motivation to regularize their life styles.

If this speculation is correct, it has encouraging connotations for the field of rehabilitation, since it could mean that the alcohol dependent, even in skid row, has not completely renounced the norms and values of the greater society though he may have deviated from its mainstream. One might infer that if the alcohol dependent has sufficient ego orientation to be selective or discriminating in his interpersonal relationships he is still capable of being motivated if his personality structure is well understood. On the other hand, it can be

Table 1

Characteristics of Subjects

Age	N	Percent
Under 25	1	1.8
25-29	0	0.0
30-34	3	5.4
35-39	5	9.1
40-44	3	5.4
45-49	8	14.5
50-54	9	16.4
55-59	11	20.0
60-64	11	20.0
65 and over	4	7.3
	55	

Race	N	Percent
Caucasian	46	83.6
Negro	8	14.6
American Indian	1	1.8
	55	

Housing	N	Percent
None	29	54.7
Room alone	20	37.7
Apartment	4	7.5
	53	

Frequency of appearance at Salvation Army South End Corps	N	Percent
Daily	33	71.7
Less than daily	13	28.3
	46	

Disability in addition to alcohol dependency	N	Percent
None	12	21.8
Acute	4	7.3
Chronic	23	41.8
Unknown	16	29.1
	55	

Table 2

Socioeconomic Background

	Father		Mother		Subject	
	N	*Percent*	*N*	*Percent*	*N*	*Percent*
Education						
Some grammar school	3	7.3	1	2.9	6	11.1
Completed grammar school	15	36.6	12	35.3	12	22.2
Some high school	5	12.2	4	11.8	13	24.1
Completed high school	10	24.4	10	29.4	11	20.4
Some education beyond high school	2	4.9	2	5.9	8	14.8
Completed college	3	7.3	2	5.9	3	5.6
Education beyond college	2	4.9	0	0	1	1.8
No formal education	1	2.4	3	8.8	0	0
	41		34		54	
Occupational Category[a]						
Professional, managerial, technical	8	15.7	6	13.6		
Clerical, sales	3	5.9	3	6.8		
Service	7	13.7	7	15.9		
Farming, fishing, forestry, etc.	2	3.9	1	2.3		
Processing	2	3.9	0	0		
Machine trades	7	13.7	1	2.3		
Bench work	2	3.9	3	6.8		
Structural work	12	23.5	0	0		
Miscellaneous	8	15.7	0	0		
Housewife	–	–	19	43.2		
Unknown	0	0	4	9.1		
	51		44			
Occupational Skill Level						
Professional, managerial	7	14.3	6	28.6		
Technical	2	4.1	0	0		
Skilled	24	49.0	4	19.0		
Semiskilled	5	10.2	4	19.0		
Unskilled	11	22.4	7	33.3		
	49		21			
Experience with Public Assistance[b]						
None	30	100.0	26	86.7		
Some	0	0	4	13.3		
	30		30			

[a]*Dictionary of Occupational Titles,* U. S. Department of Labor, 1965.

[b]During subject's childhood.

Table 3

Subjects' Present Sources of Income

Source of Income	N	Percent
Present Employment		
None or less than 1/week	36	72.0
Not employed, but works regularly 1-2/week	4	8.0
3-4/week regularly	6	12.0
33 hours or more/week	4	8.0
	50	
Employment During Past 6 Months or Since Last Full-Time Job		
None	17	31.5
Infrequent	8	14.8
1-2/week	6	11.1
3-4/week	8	14.8
Irregular but weekly	13	24.1
Nearly full-time	2	3.7
	54	
Public Welfare Assistance		
None	44	84.6
Disability assistance	3	5.8
General relief	1	1.9
Old Age Assistance	1	1.9
Unknown	3	5.8
	52	
Financial Assistance Other Than Public Welfare Assistance		
None	42	80.7
Unemployment	2	3.8
Social Security	3	5.8
Government pension	2	3.8
Government disability	1	1.9
Social Security Disability	1	1.9
Social Security and Government pension	1	1.9
	52	

Table 4

Present Motivation to Work

Work Orientation	N	Percent
Still Looking for Work		
Looking (at least once a week)	20	48.8
Not looking	9	22.0
Not looking due to disability	12	29.3
	41	
Hours Per Week Desired		
Full-time	23	74.2
Part-time	8	25.8
	31	
Knowledge of Where or How to Look for Work		
MP, LP (Manpower, Labor Pool) only	13	38.2
Employment agencies (alone or in combination)	8	23.5
Direct to employer (alone or in combination)	10	29.4
Center, friends, "They come to me."	3	8.8
	34	
How Long Ago Last Full-Time Job		
Under 6 months	12	27.9
6 month to under 1 year	6	13.9
1–2 years	8	18.6
3–5 years	9	20.9
6–10 years	2	4.6
11–15 years	5	11.6
16–20 years	0	0
21–life	1	2.3
	43	
How Long Ago Last Job		
Under 6 months	12	54.5
6 months to 1 year	3	13.6
1–2 years	2	9.1
3–5 years	5	22.7
	22	

Table 5

**Relationship Between Subject's Present
Housing and Present Financial Assistance
Other than Public Assistance**

Housing	None	Yes	Total
Room alone	13	6	19
No room	27	1	28
Total	40	7	47

Yates $\chi^2 = 4.970$, $df = 1$, $p < 0.026$

argued that those men who did not mix in the center's activities were poorer rehabilitation prospects, because their lack of social interactional skills would make entry into a treatment relationship difficult.

A major concern in the rehabilitation of any handicapped or disabled individual is his motivation to express independence through gainful employment. In this regard the rehabilitation potential of the alcohol dependent population is somewhat encouraging, or can be approached with at least cautious optimism, if we utilize current and recent work history as indicators. As indicated in Table 3, approximately 60 percent of the alcohol dependent men worked at least once a week or more during the six months prior to the interview or since their last full-time job. Thus, although their work patterns can be considered irregular, it can be inferred that some work patterns still exist which can be developed during the rehabilitation process. Moreover, attitudes toward work and earning are not totally negative.

The existence of some motivation to work is further substantiated by the findings in Table 4 which indicate that approximately 53 percent of those who look for work do not wait for work to come to them or depend only upon manpower or labor pools but, rather, formally seek work from employers or employment agencies. This pattern of formally seeking employment can be interpreted as indicating the alcohol dependent's continuing perception of himself as part of the labor force and the vocational subsystem of society.

Some limited optimism is further engendered by the findings in Table 3 which indicate that over four-fifths were independent of financial assistance from any institutionalized source to maintain

Table 6

**Relationship Between Present Housing
and Level of Participation at the Salvation Army Center**

	Housing		
Participation Level	Room Alone	No Room	Total
Minimal	10	6	16
Moderate to extensive	9	21	30
Total	19	27	46

$$\chi^2 = 4.56, df = 1, p < 0.05$$

themselves. When one couples this with the information presented in Table 2, showing that almost 87 percent of the parents of the research population had no welfare history, the absence of a generational pattern of welfare dependence suggests even greater potential for motivating the alcohol dependent for vocational rehabilitation.

Although 42 percent of the alcohol dependents reported the presence of some chronic disabling condition, such disability could hardly be delineated in general as a cause of alcohol dependency. However, in some cases, disability could serve as a subsequent contributing factor and, in other cases, a result of long-term alcohol use. If such disability causes the individual to feel inadequate and unable to compete and be productive in a society which places high value on such attributes, it might exacerbate if not cause drinking behavior. In a culture which places a premium upon perfection, physical or mental disability can cause pronounced feelings of difference and inadequacy which could contribute to increased dependency upon alcohol.

The rehabilitation of the alcohol dependent's other disabilities is a good point at which to start his total rehabilitation and can be used as a handle that is more easily accepted, particularly if the individual denies having an alcohol problem. It is quite possible that the treatment relationships which the alcohol user develops during the physical rehabilitation process can be used to motivate him in the direction of less dependency upon alcohol. It is interesting to speculate upon how many alcohol dependents not on skid row are suffering from other disabilities which contribute to or aggravate their dependence upon alcohol.

What stands out in a consideration of the characteristics of the population is that, while there is an essential homogeneity of adaptation demanded by life style, the skid-row setting does not necessarily mean homogeneity of social, psychological, and demographic background of the individuals. In the simplest sense, the characteristics of the research population of alcohol dependents can be viewed with optimism or pessimism depending upon one's viewpoint. These individuals present a paradox. On the one hand, their educational and socioeconomic backgrounds are relatively good, even during the economic depression years. Yet, the fact that their life style is at the skid-row level — many deny themselves health care and refuse to negotiate with community agencies for financial and other help — is cause for some pessimism in regard to their rehabilitation potential. What happened in the lives of these men to contribute to this situation?

.

5 Family Factors in Alcohol Dependency

Most behavioral scientists would agree that the family system is a crucial variable in the personality development of the individual. Since the family provides the individual with his major primary psychosocial relationships, to a large extent it exerts a profound influence upon what the person becomes and how he becomes that way.

If we are to achieve success in the rehabilitation of the alcohol dependent it is important to understand and, if necessary, modify the family processes which contribute to this dependency. The family is increasingly becoming a target for treatment. Social casework historically concerned itself with the family as its principal unit for treatment. Psychiatry during the past decade has become concerned with family functioning. More than ever, the field of rehabilitation is looking to work with the client's family as an important part of the rehabilitation process as reflected in the vocational rehabilitation amendments of 1968.

If the rehabilitation professional is provided with the knowledge of the possible effects of factors in the family background upon the alcohol dependent client, he is in a far better position to help the family to meet the clients' needs. If there is no available family or if the family is emotionally unable to meet the psychosocial needs of the client dependent on alcohol, then such knowledge will enable the rehabilitation worker to utilize resources in the community to reconstruct a substitute family milieu to replace nurturance and other gaps and deficiencies which existed in the client's own family environment. With this goal in view, the study was designed to investigate certain specific variables hypothesized as contributing to the development of dependency upon alcohol.

Emotional Loss

Emotional loss, real or fancied, wears many masks and is responsible for many personality disorders and behavioral difficulties. Psychiatry has learned that emotional loss is the dynamic force which underlies depression. Moreover, depression is a principal component in many failures of the individual to adapt successfully to the demands and stresses which occur in his life space. It was hypothesized that the occurrence of loss was associated with the occurrences of alcohol dependency and, perhaps, was one of the factors which contributed to its development.

In most cases emotional loss is represented by deprivation of loved ones by death, divorce, separation, illness, etc. However, loss of love objects may occur through rejection by or preoccupation of (withdrawal) the love object, even when the love object is physically present. Moreover, love objects lost need not necessarily be human; a lost job, business, or profession may have the same depressing effect.

The frequency with which loss of human love objects occurred is indicated by the "loss array" in Table 7. This array not only shows initial emotional losses but also indicates later repeated or replicated losses in the lives of these alcohol dependents.

The following material from the life history of Mr. B, one of the alcohol dependent subjects, illustrates in greater detail an emotional loss sequence:

At five years of age Mr. B was removed from his home and placed in a children's institution. His loss of parents when he was placed was probably not his first emotional loss. Although he did not communicate the events which led to removal from his home, one can speculate with some degree of certainty that he had been exposed to a family climate which was replete with psychological and social pathology, a good part of which took the form of rejection, parental withdrawal, and deprivation. This occurred during his first five years of life when love and nurturing behavior on the part of the caretakers is so important for personality development in the child.

After removal from his home (during the later part of his oedipal period when his struggles with guilt were at their height), he spent two years in a childrens' home after which, between the ages of 8 and 10, he went through a series of foster home placements with different families. He could not report the exact number. However, the number of placements indicates that he experienced serious adjustment difficulties. In addition, it is quite certain that each removal from a foster family represented another emotional loss for which there was some mourning and depression.

Finally, at age 10 he remained for an extended period with one family, the K's. His stay with the K's lasted until he was 14 years of age and was described as offering some degree of stability. Mr. and Mrs. K were between 50 and 60, and had a daughter who was a switchboard operator, and two sons who worked for the city. While living with them Mr. B's adopted name was "Tommy." Mr. B said that all children in the family were treated equally, he like their own son. He stated that, although he felt close to each of them, he usually went to Mrs. K with problems. It was Mrs. K who made most of the decisions. It would appear that Mr. B's early adolescence was spent in a matriarchal family where identification was with his foster mother rather than with his foster father who might have been able to provide an appropriate masculine role model. Leaving his home with the K's no doubt constituted another emotional loss.

Table 7
Emotional Losses

Subject	Age	Childhood Losses	Adult Losses
1	64	Placed in orphanage at age 5; various "adoptions"; multiple losses through repeated foster home placement	Divorce after 24 years of marriage "I went all to pieces then"; loss of adequacy through health (TB since age 24)
2	64	Mother died S age 7; father absent a great deal due to work (station engineer)	Wife unfaithful and left him after 15 years of marriage; 2 stillborns only; loss of 20-year job when company folded when S in his fifties
3	59	Father died S age 11	Wife unfaithful during S's service years during World War II and marriage of 17 years ended
4	58	Mother died S age 7; S and stepmother in conflict	Marriage of 9 years ended in divorce
5	30	No loss reported	Currently separated from wife and 2 children; 2 years ago had left home and teaching job in South — reported not being able to teach in Mass. without a Master's degree, even on the elementary school level (hinted at racial discrimination)
6	74	No loss reported	Loss of steeplejack trade when asphalt replaced slate during S's later years; lost three brothers by falls while slating (never married)
7	40	No loss reported	Loss of repair shop and girlfriend simultaneously; left one common-law wife; left a "reformed" prostitute after having lived with her 3 years
8	55	Father died S age 7	Marriage ended in separation after 21 years concurrent with a substantial financial loss
9	55	Parents divorced S age 6; lived alternate 6 months with each parent	Wife divorced him after 4 years of marriage due to demands made of medical doctor; lost right to practice medicine after abortion

(continued)

Table 7 (*continued*)

Subject	Age	Childhood Losses	Adult Losses
10	60	Mother died S age 6 months; father died S age 12 years	No loss reported (never married)
11	58	Father heavy drinker; parents separated S age 15; poor health and physical pain since childhood	First girlfriend died prior to marriage; second girlfriend sickly and went away to never return (never married)
12	47	Father heavy drinker; parents divorced S age 5	S returned from service to find fiancee married and pregnant (never married)
13	66	Adoptive parents rigid and overprotective; learned of adoption from children in neighborhood in traumatic way	Marriage of 2 years ended in separation; rejected by only son and not allowed to see his grandchildren
14	47	No loss reported	Marriage of 9 years ended in divorce after wife's infidelity
15	47	Mother died at S's birth; father died 2 months later; grandmother strict and punished physically	Fiancee died 2 weeks prior to marriage date; severe depression (mental breakdown) after retirement following 22 years in Army (loss of way of life) (never married)
16	35	Mother died S age 5; father in service and S did not see him for years at a time.	No loss reported (never married)
17	58	Rarely saw father; parents "estranged"	No loss reported (never married)
18	51	Parents divorced S age 15	No loss reported (never married)
19	59	Father deserted shortly after S born; mother and sister drank heavily	First childless marriage of 2 years ended in divorce after wife's infidelity; second marriage ended when wife left him after 22 years
20	61	No loss reported	No loss reported (broke up with girlfriend in order not to burden her with care of sick mother—S cared for mother until she died when S age 41)

Table 7 (*continued*)

Subject	Age	Childhood Losses	Adult Losses
21	35	Father died S age 5	Marriage ended in divorce after 2 years (S would not stop drinking and wife began seeing other men)
22	59	No loss reported	First wife died in childbirth; son had to be placed in convent
23	43	No loss reported	First wife died in childbirth after 1 year of marriage
24	47	Father "might have been considered alcoholic"	First marriage of 9 years ended in divorce; second marriage of 2 years ended in divorce when wife began running around with other men
25	55	Father alcoholic and was hospitalized and arrested for his drinking	No loss reported (never married)
26	60	No loss reported	No loss reported (never married or engaged, "not very forward with girls")
27	68	Mother died in childbirth S age 22 months; aunt and uncle raised S who saw his father 1-2/month and some of summer	Fiancee killed by lightning prior to marriage date (never married)
28	53	No loss reported	Wife died after 24 years of marriage when S age 42
29	51	No deaths or broken home; however, childhood "too painful" to discuss	Marriage ended in separation after 15 years
30	53	No loss reported	After 9 years of marriage and while S in service, wife wished to marry another and divorced S; loss of railroad job after 28 years when railroad began losing business
31	60	Father alcoholic and was abusive to family and rarely brought home money	Suicide attempts after loss of "psychopathic" wife of 16 years and loss of mother

(*continued*)

Table 7 (*continued*)

Subject	Age	Childhood Losses	Adult Losses
32	47	No loss reported	Divorce after 21 years of marriage
33	60	No loss reported	Wife left S after 28 years of marriage
34	58	No loss reported	First divorce after 9 months from woman 16 years his junior; Second divorce after 9 months of marriage whose intent was to give the child a name; job loss after 19 years
35	47	Mother died S age 13; father drank heavily	Loss of citizenship as a result of desertion in time of war (dishonorably discharged); first wife could not have children and separation finally ensued; second wife (illegal) who was 20 years S's senior died after they lived together for 2 years
36	60	Father who worked from 6 a.m. to 11 p.m. every night died S age 8	No loss reported (never married— "they all turned sour")
37	37	No loss reported	No loss reported (never married)
38	39	S weak and fragile child, hospitalized a good deal, unable to participate in athletics	Fiancee broke engagement; she did not want to be saddled with another alcoholic like her father
39	49	No loss reported	Divorced after marriage of at least 6 years
40	61	Mother died S in early teens	Lost own painting business after 30 years; only daughter died at 8 months of age; currently separated from wife after more than 22 years of marriage
41	61	Father deserted family S age 1; mother alcoholic; at age 11 S learned that aunt was not his mother and vice versa	No loss reported (never married)

Table 7 (*continued*)

Subject	Age	Childhood Losses	Adult Losses
42	30	No loss reported	S and girlfriend broke up after 8 years because S would not become Jehova Witness (never married)
43	70	Father died (S has no recollection of him)	Wife died after 13 year of marriage and no children when S age late thirties
44	60's	No loss reported	No loss reported (never married lived with mother until she died 4 years ago)
45	51	Father died S age 3	Separated from wife after 2 years of marriage (S: "the grass is always greener. . .")
46	42	No loss reported	No loss reported (never married)
47	34	Father alcoholic, violent and abusive to family and hung himself S age 7	No loss reported (never married; at age 22 S broke engagement rather than stop drinking)
48	50	No loss reported	Job loss due to injury after 25 years; a childless marriage of 11 years ended when wife had a child by another man while S in service
49	21	Father in Coast Guard and on shipboard for 3-6 months per year; father heavy drinker	No loss reported (not married)
50	52	No loss reported	Recently lost 18-year job and thrown out of house by wife after 23 years of marriage
51	50	No loss reported	No loss reported (never married; pressure from friends and family resulted in broken engagement to a girl 6 years his senior)
52	52	No loss reported	Divorced after 7 years of marriage S age 33

(continued)

Table 7 (*continued*)

Subject	Age	Childhood Losses	Adult Losses
53	57	No loss reported	No loss reported (never married; "I never had any time" — lived with parents until they died and then with aunt)
54	61	Father heavy drinker; mother died *S* age 16	First wife unfaithful after having ovaries removed after 4 years of marriage; *S* lived "part-time" for 17 years with his second wife but presently separated from her for a year—*S* cannot locate her
55	48	Father died *S* age 17	Broken marriage

When Mr. B was fourteen, his own oldest sister married and took him to live with her and her husband until he was 18 years of age at which time he entered the military service. Prior to that time Mr. B did not know that he had any brothers or sisters; from his sister he learned he had four sisters and three brothers. No one had told him how the family broke up, although he was informed that both of his parents drank. He mentioned meeting his mother every once in a while at a hotel where she worked as a "silverware woman." Both parents, however, died while he was at the childrens' institution. He reported feeling closest to his oldest sister, "even today." "She was like a mother to me." Mr. B was the youngest of eight children. His father was a coachman and his mother worked full time. Mr. B went through the seventh grade in a vocational school; he has no idea what his parents' education was.

Mr. B married when he was 19 and was divorced 24 years later (1921-1945). While in the service he never drank. There he worked in the kitchen and had dinners, banquets, etc. to prepare for the officers; and because of his duties he "just had to be sober." His drinking really increased after the divorce. "I went all to pieces then." When asked what brought the divorce on, he said he didn't really know, that drinking could have had something to do with it, business was bad at that time and he wasn't working, and it was at this time that he was sent away for nonsupport. He blamed no one but himself; he just "got discouraged." His wife never touched a drink: she was very athletic. He would like to trace his family but he has no idea where they might be; he has a son and three daughters.

Mr. B was hospitalized for TB five times for a minimum of a year each time; otherwise he has never been hospitalized. He thought school was "pretty good," but the years he spent in the Home (Catholic), although he didn't mind them, were spent in prayer. He stated that he never had time for scouts or "anything like that," although he did enjoy baseball and fights.

Thus, in evaluating the life history of Mr. B it is evident that key periods in his life were repeatedly punctuated with separation, loss of love objects, and the necessity to constantly form new object relationships. Even his five hospitalizations for tuberculosis meant separation to enter the hospital and later separation from close attachments formed with nurturing hospital staff. His loss of wife and family most likely represented final loss which resulted in his total immersion into dependency upon alcohol.

Another type of emotional loss is illustrated by material from the life history of Mr. S. This type of loss takes place not only through permanent removal but also by temporary removal or absence of love objects.

Mr. S's father was a career military man. He pointed out that as a child he would not see his father for years at a time. His mother was a full-time factory worker (lact of maternal availability) and died when the subject was 5 years of age (during the oedipal period when his father was absent; the guilt and punishment fantasies relative to his mother's death are certainly open to speculation). He stated that he did not remember his mother (repression) at all.

Mr. S reported that his father drank heavily; and, thus, paternal availability to the subject was reduced even during the periods that the father was home. The subject pointed out that he had been very close to his older brother emotionally, but as time passed his brother began to drink heavily and drifted away from him (further lack of availability of a love object). Following the death of his mother, he went to live with his paternal grandmother with whom he had a close relationship. However, there was no grandfather in the home and consequently no readily available masculine love object with which to identify. Mr. S, now 35 years of age and a moderately heavy drinker, has been arrested and incarcerated for drinking five times. (Alcohol might have provided the means by which he could compensate for feelings of inadequate masculinity.)

Death, Divorce, Separation

Parental deprivation as an etiological factor in alcohol dependency has been dealt with by a number of researchers (Floch, 1947; Straus and McCarthy 1951; Oltman et. al., 1952; Oltman & Friedman, 1953; Wahl, 1956; Martensen-Larsen, 1957; Moore and Ramseur, 1960; Hilgard and Newman, 1963; Tahka, 1966). Parental loss or deprivation has generally been used to denote the loss of one of both parents through death, divorce, or separation at or before early adulthood. On occasion loss has been conceptualized on a psychological level rather than purely a physical one, i.e., parental conflict, "mental illness." Although the proportion of parental loss varied among studies, death predominated as the cause of loss, with loss of father occurring more often than mother loss. These findings are summarized in Table 8. As may be seen, overall parental deprivation ranged from approximately one-quarter to one-half. Differences do not appear to have reflected the age chosen prior to which loss had to have occurred nor the particular group of alcohol dependents studied. Father loss appears to have occurred two to three times more frequently than mother loss, but generally included in father loss is loss through divorce or separation (loss of mother rarely occurs under these circumstances).

Table 8

Summary of Reported Statistics on Parental Deprivation
(nearest whole percent)

Investigator	N	Sex	Source	Overall Loss	Prior to Age	Cause		Parent Lost		
						Death	Divorce or Separation	Father	Mother	Both
Floch (1947)	276	M	Correctional Institution	28[a]		17	9			
Straus & McCarthy (1951)	444	M	N. Y. Bowery	50	20					
Oltman et al (1952)	200	M	State Hospital	31[b]	19	24	6	18	8	5
Oltman & Friedman (1953)	500	M & F	State Hospital	33[b]	19	24	9	20	7	6
Wahl (1956)	109	M	State Hospital	37	15	24	13	30	10	
Martensen-Larsen (1957)	518	M	Clinic	22	15			11	4	7
Moore & Ramseur (1960)	100	M	VA Hospital	45	early adol.	28	17	13	10	5
Hilgard & Newman (1963)	929	M & F	State Hospital	26	19					
Tahka (1966)	50	M	Clinic	34[c]	19	22	12	22		
Nerri (1968)	53	M	Salvation Army	47	18	34	13	15	13	6

[a] Included 2 percent parental conflict.
[b] Included 1 percent mental illness.
[c] Living mothers served as criterion for subject selection.

Table 9

Parental Deprivation by Parent Lost,
Cause of Loss, and Age of Subject
at Loss

		Age		
Loss	*0-5*	*6-12*	*13-17*	*Total*
Death of Mother	2(3.8)	2(3.8)	3(5.7)	7(13.2)
Death of Father	2(3.8)	5(9.4)	1(1.9)	8(15.1)
Death of Both	1(1.9)	2(3.8)	0(0.0)	3(5.7)
Divorce/Separation	4(7.5)	1(1.9)	2(3.8)	7(13.2)
Total	9(17.0)	10(18.9)	6(11.4)	25(47.2)

For the alcohol dependents in this study, overall deprivation prior to age 18 was 47 percent, with death the cause of 34 percent of the losses. In terms of parent lost, 13 percent experienced loss of mother; 15 percent, loss of father; and 6 percent, loss of both parents. Loss of parent or parents during the first 5 years of life occurred for 17 percent; between the ages of 6 and 12, 19 percent during adolescence, 11 percent. Loss, according to parent lost, cause of loss, and age of the subject at loss is presented in Table 9.

The capacity to form and the desire to seek sound, meaningful interpersonal relationships is unquestionably related to the nature and quality of early parent-child relationships. Although parental deprivation was considerable, its association with subsequent dependence on alcohol must be viewed with caution. More probable is the association of parental loss with subsequent vulnerability to stress situations. Alcohol dependence is but one of many possible maladaptive coping behaviors.

Birth order has also been considered a factor associated with alcohol dependence (Baken, 1949; Feeny et al., 1955; Wahl, 1956; Martensen-Larsen, 1957; Wallerstein, 1957; Navratil, 1959; Schachter, 1959; Moore and Ramseur, 1960; Smith and McIntyre, 1963; Smart, 1963; Vogel-Sprott, 1963; DeLint, 1964; Grosz, 1964; Smith, 1965; Rathod, et al., 1966; and Tahka, 1966). Earlier studies indicated a tendency toward overrepresentation of youngest children or at least later-borns in alcohol dependent populations. However, when variables such as family size and parental deprivation were taken into consideration by more recent investigators, the relationship between ordinal position and alcohol dependency became more dubious.

Frequency distributions for birth order and sibship size based on responses from the alcohol dependents in this study are presented in Tables 10 and 11. Findings similar to those reported by others were obtained when relationships among the variables family size, sibling position, and parental deprivation were investigated. Youngest children were more likely to have come from smaller families of four or fewer children ($\chi^2 = 10.94$, $df = 1$, $p < 0.001$); subjects characterized as coming from smaller families and/or occupying the position of youngest child were more likely to have lost a parent or parents. Specifically, youngest children were more likely to have experienced parental loss both prior to age 18 ($\chi^2 = 10.77$, $df = 1$, $p < 0.01$) and when parental deprivation within the first five years was controlled for ($\chi^2 = 5.06$, $df = 1$, $p < 0.05$). Alcohol dependents from smaller families of four or fewer children were more likely to have experienced parental loss both during the first five years (Yates $\chi^2 = 4.12$, $df = 1$, $p < 0.05$) and during the first twelve years of life ($\chi^2 = 5.46$, $df = 1$, $p < 0.02$).

No overrepresentation of birth order was observed when family size was controlled for (following the procedure used by Smart, 1963), although a tendency toward a preponderance of second-borns (included were 5 youngest children and 12 middle children) was noted ($\chi^2 = 4.782$, $df = 2$, $p < 0.10$, $n = 53$). Schachter's (1959) data supported the notion that first-borns are more likely to solve their problems by depending upon or affiliating with other people; later-borns are more likely to resort to nonaffiliative means, such as alcohol use, in attempting to deal with stress situations. He suggested that alcohol dependency among later-borns might represent a withdrawal reaction to stress.

Since nearly half the alcohol dependents reported parental loss prior to age 18, with three-quarters of these experiencing deprivation due to death or separation prior to adolescence, the extent to which a sibling might have substituted for a lost parent was examined. Subjects were asked if they felt particularly close to a brother or

Table 10

Sibship Size

Size	N	Percent
One	7	13.21
Two	5	9.43
Three	4	7.55
Four	11	20.75
Five	10	18.87
Six	6	11.32
Seven	2	3.77
Eight	0	0.00
Nine	4	7.55
Ten-Twelve	4	7.55
	53	

Table 11

Birth Order

Position	N	Percent
Only	7	12.96
Oldest	9	16.67
Youngest	15	27.78
Middle	23	42.59
	54	

Table 12

Sibling to Whom the Subject Felt
Closest

Sibling	N	Percent
Older sister (no other sibling present)	1	2.3
Older sister (other sibling(s) present)	11	25.6
Younger sister (no other sibling present)	0	0.0
Younger sister (other sibling(s) present)	6	14.0
Older brother (no other sibling present)	1	2.3
Older brother (other sibling(s) present)	3	7.0
Younger brother (no other sibling present)	1	2.3
Younger brother (other sibling(s) present)	6	14.0
Equally close to all	4	9.3
Close to none	8	18.6
Twin sister	1	2.3
Equally close to more than one but not all	1	2.3
	43	

sister and, if so, to which. The distribution according to brother or sister to whom the subject felt closest is presented in Table 12. As indicated in the table, regardless of whether other siblings were present or not, 28 percent of the male subjects reported feeling closer to an older sister, although the majority had another sibling available. Forty-four percent reported feeling closer to a sister (regardless of age) while only 26 percent reported feeling closer to a brother. The difference between feeling closer to an older or younger sibling was less — 37 percent reported feeling closer to an older sibling and 30 percent to a younger sibling. Interestingly, nearly a fifth did not feel close to any sibling, suggesting the possibility of an inability to form meaningful object relationships early in life.

Further analysis indicated that alcohol dependents who reported feeling closest to an older sister were more likely to have occupied the position of youngest child than that of middle child ($\chi^2 = 4.68$, $df = 1$, p H 0.05). Furthermore, a tendency to have reported feeling closest to a sibling whose age and sex characteristics predominated within the sibship was observed. Thus, probability, in terms of both the age-sex characteristics of the siblings and the subject's position within the sibship hierarchy, played an important role in determining sibling closeness.

The extent to which parental loss was a factor in determining sibling closeness was explored. It might be expected that children who lost a parent would seek to establish a substitute relationship with an older sibling of the same sex as the lost parent. No relationships were observed to indicate that siblings functioned as substitute parents. Nor was there any evidence that the alcohol dependents themselves functioned as substitute parents by providing nurturance to other siblings.

Low Parental Availability

In addition to the physical loss of one or both parents through death, divorce, or separation, parental deprivation may also be conceptualized in terms of low parental availability. Considered will be large family size and the working mother as variables which might affect maternal availability, the father whose business demands more of his time than the usual which might affect paternal availability, and excessive drinking, which might affect both maternal and paternal availability.

The Large Family. It has been suggested that children from large families may experience maternal deprivation because the mother's time and attention must be divided among so many. If this were true, one might expect children from families of five or more children to feel closer to a sister, an older sister, or possibly even an older sibling who might be nurturing. None of these relationships, however, proved significant. If dependency needs were frustrated because of lower maternal availability in larger families, the behavior did not manifest itself through a nurturing relationship with another sibling. Moreover, even when sibling position within a given family size was taken into consideration, no relationship between family size and sibling-closer-to was found.

The Working Parent. The parent is temporarily unavailable to his children when working. In the case of the working mother, she is not

Table 13

Sibling Closer to as a Function of the Working Mother

| Sibling Closer to | Working Mother | | |
	Yes	No	Total
Older sister	7	1	8
Other than older sister	6	10	16
Total	13	11	24

Fisher exact (2-tail) = 0.054

only less able to satisfy the dependency demands of each child as is the mother of a large family but she is unable to satisfy them at all when physically absent from the home. Of the forty-four subjects who were able to supply information as to the extent to which their mother worked prior to their eighteenth birthday, twenty-five reported that she did work during that period, while nineteen stated that she did not. Of the mothers who worked, over two-thirds worked full-time when employed. The majority were employed during their children's childhood and many continued to work through their adolescence. No relationship was found to exist between loss of father and the employment status of the mother. However, when the mother did work, a greater than expected proportion of subjects reported feeling closer to an older sister rather than to another sibling. This relationship is presented in Table 13.

The typical father works an eight-hour day but is usually available to his children in the evenings and on weekends. Low paternal availability as a result of excessive work demands was noted in five cases. Three fathers worked nights as well as days and two spent considerable time traveling away from the home. Although four of these five subjects had an older brother with whom to identify, only one reported feeling closer to that older brother.

The Drinking Parent. Excessive drinking on the part of one or both parents is another factor affecting parental availability. If a parent drinks to a substantial extent, the parent-child relationship might not be an adequate or meaningful one or even one that is based on reality factors. Not only might the parent-child relationship suffer in general but the process of identification might be affected, in part at least, by the ambiguities and inconsistencies in the image created by the drinking parent. Based on case history material, Newell (1950) pointed to the affectionate, kind, sober father and the indifferent, often unkind, drunk father. Another example might be the meek, mild-mannered, relatively passive father who becomes actively aggressive while under the influence of alcohol. In either case, the child is faced with the problem of integrating conflicting images.

Excessive dependency on alcohol may be conceived of as reflective of a basic weakness in the consumer, usually an inability to cope adequately with life and its stresses. In the case of a male child, if the drinking parent is the father, the child is presented with an inadequate role model with which to identify. Does the child, then, reject his father as a model on the basis of the "bad" drinking father or because of an inability to resolve the inconsistencies of a "good" sober and "bad" drinking father? Or does he incorporate the values and characteristics of the drinking father, having resolved the inconsistencies in images presented, through distortion and fantasy, or simply incorporate the characteristics of the "good" sober father who is weak?

The distribution according to parental drinking is presented in Table 14. The small percentage of mothers whose drinking was reported as heavy generally agrees with the findings of Feeney et al. (1955), Moore and Ramseur (1960), and Tahka (1966). They reported from 0 to 6 percent heavy drinking among mothers of alcoholics in their respective studies. The percentage of fathers of alcohol dependents who drank heavily in the present study is in general agreement with that reported by Feeney et al. but is considerably lower than the 35 and 38 percent reported by Moore and Ramseur and Tahka, respectively. Rathod (1966) found that nearly two-thirds of a group of clinic patients who were being treated for alcoholism had one or both parents who drank heavily whereas, in the present study, the proportion was approximately one-quarter.

In that only two out of twenty-nine mothers drank heavily and none moderately, involvement with alcohol by the mother generally did not affect the mother-child relationship. On the other hand, half of the father (21 out of 41) drank moderately to heavily. Jackson and Connor (1953) considered the extent to which parents drank of

Table 14

Parental Drinking

Extent of Drinking	Mother		Father	
	N	Percent	N	Percent
Not at all	12	40.0	6	13.0
Socially	8	26.7	8	17.4
Moderately	0	00.0	10	21.7
Heavily	2	6.7	11	23.9
Not heavily (or no history of alcoholism in family)	7	23.3	6	13.0
Unknown	1	3.3	5	10.9
	30		46	

less consequence than the extent to which their attitudes toward drinking differed. They found that parents of alcohol dependents disagreed markedly in their attitudes toward the use of alcohol while both parents of nondrinkers or social drinkers either disapproved of or permitted moderate drinking.

The effect of the drinking father on the father-son relationship was not ascertained by this study. However, in the absence of adequate parental figures, the superego often fails to develop properly and object relations tend to remain at the narcissistic level. The lack of a person with whom to identify may result in a self-sufficient individual but one with no internalized conscience. The child, and later the adult, can love only himself. In the case of an inadequate father figure, the result might be an incomplete masculine identification and a pronounced infantile dependency on the mother. According to Navratil (1959), the alcohol dependent does, in fact, identify to a greater extent with his mother than with his father.

These findings suggest the necessity of making available masculine role models within the framework of the rehabilitation process. These role models can serve as "central significant figures" in the lives of the alcohol dependent males. Opportunities exist within the scope of the rehabilitation process for a number of different

Table 15

Parent to Whom Subject Felt Closer

Both Parents present	N	Percent
Mother	23	56.1
Father	2	4.9
Equally close to both	6	14.6
Close to neither	2	4.9
Parent(s) absent		
Mother (father absent)	4	9.8
Father (mother absent)	1	2.4
Parent substitute (both absent)	2	4.9
Parent substitute (one absent)	1	2.4
	41	

rehabilitation workers to become such masculine role models. Rehabilitation counselors, sheltered workshop instructors and supervisors, house father, social workers, various physical rehabilitation specialists, and others can help fill this need for the alcohol dependent.

Dynamics of Interpersonal Relationships Within the Family

In order to further assess the relationship between parent and child, data pertaining to the parent to whom the subject felt closer and, in turn, the child to whom the parent expressed particular preference were obtained. The distribution according to parent to whom the child felt closer is presented in Table 15. Excluded from statistical analysis were those subjects who felt closer to one parent when the other parent was absent or to a parent substitute when one or both

Table 16

Parents' Favorite Child as Perceived by the Subject

Favorite Child	Mother (N = 27)		Father (N = 17)	
	N	Percent	N	Percent
All equally favored	10	37.0	10	58.8
Subject	9	33.3	0	0.0
Older brother	2	7.4	1	5.9
Older sister	2	7.4	1	5.9
Older pseudo-sib	0	0.0	0	0.0
Younger brother	1	3.7	1	5.9
Younger sister	3	11.1	3	17.6
Younger pseudo-sib	0	0.0	1	5.9

29.6

42.1

Table 17

Decision Making Within the Family of
Orientation

Decision Maker	N	Percent
Shared by both parents	11	22.9
Mother (father present)	11	22.9
Father (mother present)	16	33.3
Mother (father absent)	10	20.8
	48	

parents were absent. No variables introduced thus far were found to be significantly associated with the parent to whom the child felt closer.

The distributions of responses according to the favorite child of the mother and of the father as perceived by the subject are presented in Table 16. It will be noted that not a single subject in seventeen reported that he was his father's favorite, whereas one-third of twenty-seven subjects reported being their mother's favorite. It has been said that as a child the alcohol dependent was "spoiled" by his mother. Navratil (1959) found that one-half of his 600 subjects perceived themselves as their mother's favorite. Of the seventeen subjects for which both parents' favorites were ascertainable, an all-or-none phenomenon was observed. Perfect agreement between fifteen sets of parents was found, or at least as perceived by the subjects: Ten sets of parents displayed no favoritism, while five sets favored a child other than the subject (Yates $\chi^2 = 10.80$, $df = 1$, $p < 0.01$).

Many researchers have characterized mothers of alcohol dependents as indulgent, protective, and spoiling, and fathers as aggressive, dominating, and severe. Others have described mothers as domineering, possessive, and controlling, and fathers as passive, dependent, and aloof. If these descriptions are relatively accurate, one might expect that the majority of subjects would point to one parent or to the other as the dominant figure in the household. To the extent that decision making provides a measure of parental dominance, subjects were asked whom they perceived to be responsible for financial, disciplinary, and other decisions involving the family. The distribution of responses is presented in Table 17.

Table 18

Decision Making and Mother's Favorite
Child

| | Decision Maker | | |
Mother's Favorite Child	Father or Shared	Mother	Total
No favorite or subject favored	12	2	14
Other than subject	1	5	6
Total	13	7	20

Yates $\chi^2 = 6.03$, $df = 1$, $p < 0.02$

If decision making does reflect parental dominance, no particular pattern emerged when both parents were present, although in the majority of families one parent did assume major responsibility. The mother was perceived as the dominant figure in slightly more than one-fifth of the cases. However, when the mother was forced to "wear the pants" because of an absent father, the percentage increased to 44. The father, when both parents were present, was the reported decision maker in 33 percent of the families.

Although no relationship was observed between decision making and sibling position when both parents were present, the to-be-expected overrepresentation of youngest children in families where the mother was forced to make decisions was observed ($\chi^2 = 21.198$, $df = 6$, $p < 0.002$). Also related to decision making was the favorite child of the mother. When the mother was perceived as the dominant figure, she was also perceived as favoring a child other than the subject (see Table 18). In these instances, the mother might be characterized as both dominating and rejecting.

Early Social Experiences

Alcohol dependency can be considered, in part, a social phenomenon, stemming at least partially from undeveloped or inadequately developed social interaction skills during childhood. The adult may discover that alcohol serves to facilitate interpersonal relationships and thus uses alcohol to compensate for this early social learning

Table 19

Participation in Boyhood Activities

Number of Activities	N	Percent
None	4	8.00
One	13	26.00
Two	11	22.00
Three	10	20.00
Four and more	12	24.00
	50	

deficit. In order to learn something about the early social competence of the alcohol dependents, subjects were asked about activities in which they participated outside of the home during their childhood and about their feelings toward school. Table 19 indicates the number of activities participated in; activities included scouts, camp, music lessons, sports, "playing with the neighborhood kids," etc. A full third participated minimally in social learning experiences outside of the home.

It was hoped that feelings toward school would indirectly reflect the degree of satisfaction obtained from peer-group interaction. Specifically, if attitudes toward school were positive, it might be assumed that social relationships were gratifying; conversely, if attitudes were negative, it might be assumed that social relationships were minimal and/or unrewarding. In addition to feelings of social competence or incompetence in the school setting are feelings of academic competence or incompetence. Feelings of self-worth, whatever the source, are important in establishing one's sense of identity and in serving later as a foundation for meeting and coping with life's demands. Table 20 shows that half the alcohol dependents expressed nonpositive feelings toward school, possibly indicating deficiencies in social and/or academic skills.

Since the school setting constitutes the individual's first major confrontation with authority and opportunity for social transactions in peer groups, the inability to meaningfully relate to the school

Table 20

Feeling Toward School

Feeling	N	Percent
Positive	23	50.0
Negative	20	43.5
Ambivalent	3	6.5
	46	

Table 21

Social Activities by Decision Making

	Decision Maker		
Number of Activities	Shared or Father	Mother	Total
None or one	3	12	15
Two to four or more	20	8	28
Total	23	20	43

$$\chi^2 = 10.39, df = 1, p < 0.01$$

setting may further decrease the likelihood of experiencing meaningful constructive social relationships. If a defect in social interaction skills continues into adulthood, the result may be further non-affiliative behavior. Dependence upon alcohol is one means of reducing the tension which accompanies social interaction or of avoiding social relationships altogether.

Findings indicated that in families in which both parents were present and the mother was perceived as making all the decisions, subjects reported engaging in minimal formal or informal activity outside the home (Table 21). Such evidence points out one negative effect of maternal dominance upon the individual's social development during early psychosocial maturation. Atypical, but illustrative, is the following life history excerpt:

Mr. M was 5 years old when his parents were divorced. . . . Frank's mother had no education and could not speak English. She had arrived from Portugal a few years before Mr. M was born. Because of this, he stated that his mother always kept him very close to her. When she would go to the store, Mr. M always went with her — as interpreter. She did not like him to attend school and, as a result, influenced his leaving classes . . . she was never abusive to him since he was the favorite child. Mr. M did not feel close to his brother and insinuated that his mother monopolized his relations with other children. . . . He stated that he did not participate in school activities or scouts because he was needed at home. He did not like school . . . he had trouble learning English since Portuguese was always spoken at home. He often skipped classes but felt this was a result of his mother's influence, not his lack of interest.

Summary of Results

It must be concluded on the basis of this data as well as that obtained by other investigators that birth order and family size are not associated per se with subsequent dependency on alcohol. That is not to say that these variables in combination with other factors might not precipitate dependency. The relationship between parental loss and ordinal position within the family is less conclusive.

Parental loss was interpreted both specifically and generally: specifically, in terms of permanent physical loss as a result of death, desertion, divorce, or separation; broadly, in terms of lower availability as a result of large family size, vocational demands, and excessive drinking. Youngest children experienced parental loss through death or separation significantly more often than did children occupying other sibling positions, even when early loss was controlled for. Similarly, subsequent alcohol dependents came significantly more often from smaller families in which parental loss occurred even when loss was controlled for up to the onset of adolescence. In other words, parental loss occurred more often than expected to youngest children and within small families.

Low paternal availability was evident in a substantial number of families in which the father was absent and/or drank excessively. However, there was no indication that paternally deprived subjects identified more closely with an older brother as a substitute father. When these data are coupled with the findings that in 44 percent of the homes the mother was the perceived or real authority figure, that social activities outside of the home were limited for the future alcohol dependent in homes in which the mother dominated, and that these men reported feeling closer to their mother than to their father in most cases when both parents were present, complete or even adequate masculine identification is questionable. Finally, no one subject reported that he was his father's favorite, while two-fifths indicated preference was given to another sibling.

The findings suggest that the alcohol dependent experienced a decreased opportunity for masculine identification with their fathers and an increased tendency to be close to and possibly controlled by their mothers. Some mothers might have fostered a level of dependency so high that the subject's only means of achieving emotional security was through closeness to the mother while remaining in the home. When these findings are coupled with the fact that such mothers are a factor in reducing the subject's childhood social experiences in the community, factors which might contribute to alcoholic dependency begin to emerge: namely, the need for the alcohol dependent to drink to reduce tensions surrounding his lack of capacity for social interaction or his need to compensate for a lack of social satisfactions and feelings of masculinity.

Implications for Rehabilitation

If the family data on the alcohol dependent is viewed from the standpoint of rehabilitation needs, a principal task becomes the replacement of emotional loss suffered in the course of early childhood development. In many cases of deprivation supportive love and nurturance were at best deficient and at worst lacking altogether. In most treatment situations rehabilitation workers are regarded as parent figures. In the case of the alcohol dependent this role of parent surrogate should be greatly emphasized. Whatever the rehabilitation setting, a "family" type of love and acceptance must pervade the treatment relationship.

Since the family backgrounds of the alcohol dependents have provided little in the way of opportunity for the development of interpersonal or social skills, the rehabilitation process must help the client acquire these skills. Some facility in the use of such skills can enable the alcohol dependent to reduce the tensions of living. He can thus rely less upon alcohol for support and retreat less into an alcohol dependent state to avoid the pain of dealing with social situations with which he is psychosocially unequipped to cope.

The use of group techniques and a knowledge of group dynamics and group therapeutic processes are vital rehabilitation aids in helping the alcohol dependent deal with possible feelings of unworthiness and inadequacy which may have resulted from the love losses that occurred in his early family life. Group experiences can also serve to provide the client with practice in the development of the social negotiative skills he may so desperately need.

The use of group rehabilitation counseling could be another valuable aid in helping the alcohol dependent feel a family-like support while simultaneously gaining skill and confidence in the social negotiative areas. Auxiliary rehabilitation personnel (rehabilitation aids) might be used as participant observers or as discussion leaders in these counseling groups to record process or to act as interactional catalytic agents in and precipitate situations whereby, with the support of the group, the alcohol dependent could become more secure in his ability to successfully exercise social skills in a milieu of controlled emotional stress and demands. Within the feeling context of such a counseling group, role-playing episodes designed to strengthen the alcohol dependent's social negotiative skills can be carried out. Margolin (1955) demonstrated encouraging success in his design of role-playing episodes for this purpose with severely disturbed psychotic patients, some of whom also had alcohol problems.

Findings do not seem to support the use of potentially traumatic group techniques such as "encounter" or "confrontation" group methods whereby the family type support of the group may be temporarily withdrawn. The emotional losses in the early life of the alcohol dependent in combination with his poor social negotiative skills make his tolerance for this type of stress inadequate and could result in the exacerbation of his drinking behavior. Modified sensitivity techniques, however, can be attempted with the alcohol dependent, but he must at all times (at least during the initial phases of his treatment) be protected from the total hostility or rejection of the (family) group. Such an encounter would merely serve to replicate or recapitulate the emotional loss pattern which the data show has already been replicated and elicit the repetition compulsion whose major expression is in drinking behavior.

Community psychiatry during the past ten years has been carrying out some interesting experimentation in the treatment of the alcohol dependent. The field of rehabilitation could profitably borrow the use of the community "caretaker concept," pioneered by Lindemann et al. (1963) and Caplan (1961). Using this concept, the rehabilitation professional responsible for the coordination of services for the alcohol dependent client could enlist the aid of certain key individuals in the community social system who interface with the alcohol dependent in the social systems which effect his daily living. Such people as clergymen, policemen, probation officers and their assistants, recreational workers, welfare workers, etc. could be called upon during times of crisis to maintain the rehabilitation progress of the alcohol dependent. These community caretakers should be oriented toward giving the type of support and encouragement typical of an understanding and compassionate family member. This would not negate their using their legitimated community authority to motivate conformity or controlled drinking behavior.

Our findings suggest that in the case of the severe alcohol dependent whose history shows much family deprivation and emotional loss the feasibility of the "constructed group" might be explored. This technique involves a special therapy group which is constructed around the individual being treated or rehabilitated to meet his specific needs and is led by a trained helping professional. This method of treatment has been successfully used with emotionally disturbed children. Naturally, other members of the group benefit from the experience as well as the individual for whom the group is constructed. The purpose of the group, in the case of the alcohol dependent, would be to provide him with a substitute family within which he could learn to experience an acceptable dependent relationship so that he could learn to depend upon people rather than alcohol to help him cope with the tension and demands of life.

Whatever group rehabilitation treatment method is used, it must provide ample opportunity for the male alcohol dependent to build up his masculine identification. This factor cannot be over-emphasized. Another rehabilitation goal concommitant with building up the masculine component of the alcohol dependent's personality functioning is to help him develop his capacity to compete in a socially acceptable manner. One of the major motivators in the American culture is the value of competition; in some alcohol dependents this ability has been impaired. This goal should be achieved in the context of an individual indentification with a role model in treatment as well as in psychosocial transactions which take place in his group experience.

The findings support the concept that the rehabilitation of the alcohol dependent is a community-oriented process. Although the process of alcohol dependency may receive its start within the family, it immediately becomes community linked. The dynamics of the subject's family environment interfere with the normal process of social-skills development and the ability to cope with stresses which ensue in the community social system. Therefore, the rehabilitation of the alcohol dependent is highly related to the capacity of the community to provide the milieu for his reeducation in the social negotiative function.

The utilization of the resources and institutions of the community to achieve this end should become a dynamic process. Religious institutions can provide some of the warm family-type acceptance the client may never have received; community centers and other social group work agencies can deploy the group process to provide the alcohol dependent client with goal-oriented, controlled types of social experiences to enable him to achieve the social skills and confidence which he may desperately need in order to move back into the community mainstream. Adult education institutions in the community can provide an opportunity for a positive educational experience for those alcohol dependent clients whose early experiences with school were negative, etc.

Perhaps the major point to be underscored is that frequently, because of his deviance, society denies the alcohol dependent the very ingredient he requires to become rehabilitated — acceptance. In most areas of the community the alcohol dependent is still regarded as deviant, weak, hopeless, and for the most part undesirable. Even most social welfare agencies regard the alcohol dependent as generally nonamenable to treatment. The only rehabilitation program which has a chance for success is one which reintroduces him, with adequate support, into the mainstream of the society. Rehabilitation workers, through participating in community interpretational work and planning and organizational processes, must encourage an open community for the rehabilitation of the client dependent upon alcohol.

6

Marriage and the Alcohol Dependent

The institution of marriage represents an important, if not the most important, adult primary group affiliation. Through the close and interpersonal nature of the marital relationship, many needs of the individual are fulfilled, e.g., security, companionship, mutual dependence, stability, and parenthood. To a greater extent than secondary group memberships, however, primary group associations involve considerable responsibility and sharing. To the well-socialized, emotionally mature individual the rewards of marriage far outweigh the sacrifices required. But to the individual who is unwilling or unable to commit himself to such a demanding relationship, the disadvantages seem to outweigh the advantages. He is the socially and emotionally immature individual frustrated by failure earlier in life to form meaningful interpersonal relationships.

The family functions as an early major socializing agent. One of its roles is to provide the child with the appropriate social skills necessary for obtaining maximum need satisfaction through interpersonal and intergroup relationships. The child's first meaningful interpersonal relationship is with his mother. If this relationship is unsatisfactory to the child, he may later be unwilling to become involved in other interpersonal relationships for fear of pain, frustration, or failure. On the other hand, if the relationship with the mother is too rewarding, the child may not feel the need for interaction with others. Illustrative is the child of the overindulgent, overprotective mother. The orally dependent individual is characterized by passivity, a desire to take in or to receive, a need to be succored; he is unable to give in return.

Even if an individual has successfully dealt with the problems presented during the oral stage of development, attempts to form meaningful object relations might also be hindred if the subsequent developmental stages are not met with successfully. Heterosexual relationships may be impaired by inadequate progression through the anal and phallic stages of personality development. If the Oedipal conflict is not satisfactorily resolved, the result may be incomplete masculine identification. Others have suggested that the poor adjustment to marriage made by many alcohol dependents may be traced back to these earlier stages of development.

Until two decades ago, the alcohol dependent was generally thought to be a socially unstable individual. Evidence was based largely upon the marital status of homeless men, most of whom had never entered into a single marital relationship. Of those who did marry, the vast majority reported a broken marriage (Solenberger, 1911; Laubach, 1916; Anderson, 1923; Sutherland and Locke, 1936; Straus, 1946; Straus and McCarthy, 1951). These so-called marginal members of society were described first by Bacon (1944) as undersocialized. They were said to have participated minimally in the surrounding culture and to have sought a way of life which called for minimal personal responsibility. Feelings of well-being were achieved through excessive use of alcohol.

During the 1940s and 1950s groups of arrested inebriates and those sentenced to terms in correctional institutions and workhouses for public drunkenness or crimes directly related to the use of alcohol were investigated (Bacon and Roth, 1943; Bacon, 1944; Wenger, 1944; Floch, 1947; Feeney et al., 1955; Terry et al., 1957; Pittman and Gordon, 1958; Swenson and Davis, 1959). Again, a tendency not to marry was observed but not to the extent that was found among homeless men. The rate of broken marriages, however, remained high. Although not necessarily homeless, these groups, simply because of their involvement in crimes against society, could also be labeled undersocialized. Their maladaptive behavior reflects minimal use of social groups through which socially acceptable means for obtaining need satisfactions are achieved.

However, the image of the alcohol dependent as a socially unstable individual began to decline with the advent of studies utilizing hospital and clinic groups (Barrett, 1943; Malzberg, 1947; Malzberg, 1949; Prout et al., 1950; Hochwald, 1951; Shaw, 1951; Straus and Bacon, 1951; McCullough, 1952; Walcott and Straus, 1952; Feeney et al., 1955; Falkey and Schneyer, 1957; Selzer and Holloway, 1957; Wallerstein et al., 1957; Wellman et al., 1957; Maxwell et al., 1958; Wolf, 1958; Thomas et al., 1959; Lolli et al., 1960; Moore and Ramseur, 1960; Zax and Biggs, 1961; Locke, 1962; Moon and Patton, 1963; Rossi et al., 1963; Mayer et al., 1965; Tahka, 1966). The tendency to marry was generally found to approximate that of the general population. The marriage casualty rate, although substantially higher than that of the general population, ranging from 30 to 50 percent, did not even begin to approach that observed for the homeless and arrested populations. The assumed middle and upper-middle class clinic and hospital groups exhibited a desire to enter into the permanent interpersonal relationship of marriage, although their ability to maintain such a relationship proved insufficient. The reader is referred to Bailey (1961) for an excellent review of alcohol dependency and marriage up to the sixties.

The skid-row alcohol dependent, with which the present study deals, is generally, but not necessarily, homeless and has usually been arrested at least once for public intoxication. On this basis one might expect to find characteristics among men on skid row similar to those of the homeless and arrested groups. Katz (1966) observed that the tendency to marry among nearly 2000 Salvation Army inebriates approximated that of the general population but found that, of those who did marry, over 90 percent had since dissolved their marriages. Blumberg et al. (1966) and Wilbur et al. (1966) reported relatively large proportions who had either never married or were no longer married. The marital history of this study's group of skid-row alcohol dependents is presented in Table 22. Forty-two percent never married; of those who did marry, the marriage casualty rate was extremely high. Divorce or separation contributed to the majority of broken first marriages; the total percentage of broken first marriages was brought to 100 when the widowed were added. The marriage casualty rate was observed to be comparable to that among those found in earlier studies involving arrested or homeless groups.

The Bachelor

Fourteen of the twenty-three men who had never married voluntarily reported whether or not they had ever seriously considered marriage. Of these, eleven reported having had at one time plans to marry. Their premarital relationships were terminated for the following reasons: death of fiancee, 3; fiancee married another while the subject was away in the service, 2; fiancee terminated the relationship because of the subject's drinking, 2; subject terminated the relationship because of a religious difference, 1; subject terminated the relationship because of family pressure (his fiancee was six years older than he), 1; subject terminated more than one relationship because the girl drank even more than he did, 1. Of the remaining three subjects who reported no previous marriage plans, one reported living at home with his parents until their death and then with his aunt.

For the seven men whose relationships were terminated by the

Table 22

Marital History ($N = 55$)

Marital history	N	Percent
Never Married	23	41.8
Once Married	25	45.5
Divorced	12	21.8
Separated	5	9.1
Widowed	2	3.6
Divorced or separated	6	10.9
Twice Married	7	12.7
Twice divorced	2	3.6
Once divorced — now separated	2	3.6
Widowed — now separated	1	1.8
Once divorced — now widowed	1	1.8
Once widowed — now actively married	1	1.8

death of their fiancee or by the fiancees themselves, five had experienced prior object loss through the death of a parent or through the divorce or separation of their parents. For the four men who themselves terminated the relationships, prior parental loss was experienced by only one. No relationship was found between the tendency to marry and parental loss during childhood; in other words, those who remained bachelors experienced the loss of a parent to the same degree as did those who eventually married.

The Married Man

The mean and median categories for age at first marriage was 25-27 years old. Half of the subjects entered into their first marital relationship between the ages of 23 and 27, with one quarter marrying prior to age 23 and one quarter after age 27. The mean and median category for length of marriage was 6-10 years. Forty-two percent had been married for the first time from six to fifteen years, with 29 percent married less than six years and 29 percent married from sixteen to over twenty-five years. Distributions for age at and length of first marriage are presented in Tables 23 and 24 respectively. Seven of the thirty-two men who had married reported a second marriage; however, because of the small number, second marriages will not be discussed.

The mean category for number of children from first marriages was two; the median category for number of children was one. Nearly one-fifth of the marriages involved no children. Only one-third of the marriages produced more than two children. The distribution according to number of children from the first marriage is presented in Table 25. Having and raising children carries certain responsibilities and sacrifices. That over 50 percent of the subjects reported having had only one child or no children at all suggests that they might have felt incapable of meeting or even been unwilling to meet these additional demands. (Taking, rather than giving or sharing, is a characteristic commonly attributed to dependent persons.) Not ascertained was the wife's feelings about children and this aspect should not be ignored in formulating ideas pertaining to the size of the family of procreation.

The number of children from the first marriage was found to be associated with the length of that marriage as shown in Table 26. That fewer children were found to be related to shorter marriages suggests two possible explanations for the relatively early termination of these marriages. One is simply that these subjects could not cope with the demands and responsibilities of children; the second is that these subjects might never have experienced a strong sense of "family" with, for the most part, just one child or no children at all.

Life might be conceptualized as a series of decisions. An adult who has not as yet married is primarily responsible only to himself. But once he has entered into a marital relationship, he becomes responsible not only to himself but also to his family for his actions. He must take into consideration the consequences of his decisions upon those around him. Since marriage is considered to be a partnership, decisions are no longer his alone to make; they are to be shared. However, in only about one-third of the marriages reported in this study were decisions pertaining to financial, disciplinary, and other family matters shared by both partners. In two-thirds of the

Table 23

Age of Subject at Time of First Marriage

Age of Subject	N	Percent
Under 17	0	0.0
17-19	2	7.1
20-22	5	17.9
23-24	6	21.4
25-27	8	28.6
28-30	4	14.3
31-35	2	7.1
36 and over	1	3.6
	28	

Table 24

Length of First Marriage

Length	N	Percent
Under 1 year	1	3.2
1-2 years	6	19.4
3-5 years	2	6.4
6-10 years	9	29.0
11-15 years	4	12.9
16-20 years	2	6.4
21-25 years	5	16.1
Over 25 years	2	6.4
	31	

Table 25

Number of Children from the First
Marriage

Number of children	N	Percent
0	6	18.8
1	11	34.4
2	4	12.5
3-4	10	31.2
5-6	1	3.1
7 or over	0	0.0
	32	

Table 26

Length of First Marriage and Number of Children From That Marriage

	Length of First Marriage		
Number of Children from First Marriage	Under 11 years	11 years or more	Total
0-2	15	5	20
3-7+	3	8	11
Total	18	13	31

Yates χ^2 = 4.82, df = 1, $p < 0.05$

marriages, then, the data point to a lack of sharing, a lack of involvement, responsbility, and initiative on the part of one of the partners. About one-quarter of the subjects were depended upon by their wives while one-third depended upon their wives for making the majority of decisions involving the family. The distribution according to decision maker during the first marriage is presented in Table 27.

Table 27

Decision Maker During First Marriage

Decision Maker	N	Percent
Subject and wife	6	31.6
Subject	5	26.3
Wife	6	31.6
In-law(s)	2	10.5
	19	

It will be noted that the distribution is based on nineteen of the thirty-two marriages reported.

Wives of alcohol dependents have been described as oftentimes motherly, usually dominant (Navratil and Wien, 1957). Because of his need for dependence, the alcohol dependent often chooses or is chosen by a dominant female who may serve as a substitute for a mother who may have either deprived or overgratified her child's earlier dependency strivings. DeSaugy (1962) in his study of 100 couples noted that over half the wives of alcohol dependents were dominant in marriage from the start. Lemert (1962) observed a greater frequency of dominant wives for alcohol dependents whose dependency on alcohol was evident prior to or at the time of marriage, suggesting earlier under- or overgratification of dependency needs. Although one-third of the subjects in this study reported that their spouse was primarily responsible for decision making, no relationship was found between the onset of problem drinking and decision making.

The Role of Early Family and Social Experiences

Whether a subject married or remained a bachelor did not prove to be associated with his parents' marital history, loss of a parent through death, divorce or separation, feeling closer to his mother, or being his mother's favorite child. Subjects were, however, more likely

Table 28

Relationship Between Decision Making During First Marriage and Working Status of Mother

	Decisions During First Marriage		
Working Status of Mother	Made by Other Than Subject	Made by Subject	Total
Worked	1	6	7
Housewife	3	0	3
Total	4	6	10

Fisher exact (2-tail) = 0.06

Table 29

Relationship Between Age of Subject at Time of Parental Loss and Decision Making During First Marriage

Decision Maker During First Marriage	Age of Subject at Time of Parental Loss		
	0-5	6-17	Total
Other than subject	0	3	3
Subject	3	1	4
Total	3	4	7

Fisher exact (2-tail) - 0.03

to assume primary responsibility for making the decisions in their marriage both when their mothers worked during their childhood and when they experienced parental loss prior to age 6. The implication is that early independence training, in some form, contributed to the development of a self-sufficient, autonomous individual who has learned how to take initiative and assume responsibility. These relationships are presented in Tables 28 and 29, respectively. Decision maker in the family of procreation was not found to be related to decision maker in the family of orientation.

Subjects who reported having had positive feelings toward school tended to marry rather than remain single (see Table 30). Another indicator of success in earlier personal and social relationships is the extent of participation in school, athletic, and other such activities. Again, subjects who participated in the greater number of activities as youths were significantly more likely to have married than were those who participated minimally. In addition, the greater degree of socialization associated with participation in social activities outside of the home was found to be significantly related to a more stable marital history as reflected by the length of marriage. These relationships are presented in Tables 31 and 32.

The Broken Marriage

Factors contributing to the dissolution of the first marriage are presented in Table 33. The three major reasons given were: (1) infidelity, (2) drinking, and (3) drinking in combination with other factors. The largest single reason given was infidelity on the part of the wife and occurred 3.5 times more frequently than infidelity on the part of the subject. Sexual maladjustment or inability to successfully relate heterosexually, if in fact the case, might be expected to derive from incomplete identification with the father. However, in only half of these cases could the father be considered absent as a result of death, divorce, excessive work demands, or excessive drinking.

Whether drinking was the cause or result of problems within the marital relationship was not ascertained. However, marital discord brought about by excessive drinking was reported by slightly over half the subjects; this is independent of and must not be confused with factors contributing to the divorce or separation. For the cases where drinking tended to *cause* problems, it would seem that the antisocial act of excessive drinking was more rewarding than the maintenance of meaningful object relationships involving wife and children. On the other hand, if drinking was the *result* of an unhappy home life, a maladaptive solution to the problem was chosen. Whether a cause or result, the bottle was chosen as a partial substitute for or replacement of an ungratifying human object relationship.

Forty-four percent of the subjects placed the entire blame for failure in marriage upon themselves, thereby reflecting the feelings of

Table 30

**Relationship Between Feeling Toward
School and Tendency to Marry**

Feeling Toward School	Tendency to Marry		Total
	Bachelor	Married	
Positive	7	16	23
Not positive	12	8	20
Total	19	24	43

Yates χ^2 = 3.81, df = 1, $p < 0.06$

Table 31

**Boyhood Activities and
Tendency to Marry**

Tendency to Marry	Boyhood Activities		Total
	0-1	2-4	
Bachelor	11	11	22
Married	6	22	28
Total	17	33	50

Yates χ^2 = 4.46, df = 1, $p < .05$

self-debasement and unworthiness often attributed to alcohol dependents. On the other hand, 22 percent assumed none of the blame. Finally, one-third appeared to have more realistically assessed the situation and accepted some of the responsibility for failure and placed the remainder elsewhere. Subjects who fathered more than two children did not blame only themselves for failure in marriage (Yates χ^2 = 5.57, df = 1, $p < .02$). These men had related to marriage closely enough to father three or more children and participate in the cooperative relationship of child rearing and, consequently, may have held a more positive self-concept. Seven of the thirty-two alcohol dependents who married once remarried, thus indicating a willingness

Table 32

**Length of First Marriage and
Activities as a Youth**

Activities as a Youth	Length of First Marriage		Total
	Under 11 Years	11 Years or More	
1-2	10	3	13
3 and more	4	9	13
Total	14	12	26

Yates $\chi^2 = 3.869$, $df = 1$, $p < 0.049$

Table 33

**Factors Attributed to the Dissolution
of the First Marriage ($N = 24$)**

Factors	N	Percent
Infidelity		
Subject's infidelity	1	4.2
Wife's infidelity	7	29.2
	8	33.4
Drinking		
Subject's drinking	3	12.5
Subject's and wife's		
drinking	2	8.3
	5	20.8
Subject's Drinking in Combination with		
Subject's infidelity	1	4.2
In-law interference	1	4.2
Financial problems	3	12.5
	5	20.8
In-law interference	2	8.3
Other	4	16.7

Table 34

Time Lapse Since Dissolution of Pre-
vios Marriage

Time Lapse	N	Percent
1-5 years	5	19.2
6-10 years	8	30.8
11-20 years	6	23.1
21-years and over	7	26.9
	26	

to again attempt a meaningful marital relationship in spite of a previous failure or loss.

The time lapse since the dissolution of the last marriage varied from one to over twenty-one years. The distribution is presented in Table 34. Frequencies are evenly divided between 10 years and under and over 10 years. Slightly over one-half (52 percent) of the subjects reported remaining completely out of touch with their family of procreation; the remainder maintained minimal contact. This was found not to be associated with the time lapse since the dissolution of the marriage, the number or presence or absence of children, length of the marriage, or any other factor pertaining to the marriage.

Summary

The skid-row alcohol dependents in this study evidenced both a high proportion of nonmarriage and an extremely high proportion of broken marriages through divorce or separation. It may seem, then, that these men were either unable or unwilling to commit themselves to the demands of an interpersonal relationship with the opposite sex and the responsibilities of a family; or, once having committed themselves, they were unable to maintain such a commitment. Whether the latter was primarily a function of a deficiency in level of prior personal or social adjustment or whether this deficiency brought about an excessive use of alcohol as a substitute reward for the unattainable through human object relationships is unknown. Not to be overlooked, however, are the substantial number of men who were able to function within and maintain the marital relationship for many years.

Those who did enter into marriage were more likely to have acquired earlier in life some of the social skills necessary for the formation and maintenance of interpersonal relationships (more extensive participation in neighborhood, school, church, athletic, and club activities; positive feelings toward school). Moreover, those who not only entered into marriage but were able to maintain the relationship over the years were more likely to have been those who became involved in activities outside the home in which qualities such as leadership, a sense of fair play, competencies in specific areas, and, most important, the ability to "get along" may be acquired. An early social-experience hypothesis becomes relevant, since a lack of rewarding social transactions in the community during childhood may lead to social incapacity which may produce anxiety and defects in the development of human interaction patterns which, in turn, contribute to marital instability.

Early independence training, albeit circumstantial, was related to decision making in marriage. Specifically, early parental loss and the working mother were factors in the family of the alcohol dependent which related to his subsequent perception of self as the organizationally, if not emotionally, dominant figure in the marriage. What, in reality, amounts to deprivation could have been the force which allowed for the early learning of responsibility and contributed to an adequate self-concept and sense of competency. Not to be overlooked is the importance of a sense of masculinity which can, at least in part, be derived from being relied upon as the authority on discipline, finances, and other matters involved in family living.

Not to be neglected are early family factors *not* associated with the tendency to marry or marital stability. As will be recalled, the stability of the parents' marital history and, when this was unstable, the age of the subject at which parental loss occurred, closeness to mother, and mother's favorite child all bore no relationship to the tendency to marry or remain single. Loss of one or both parents, especially at an early age or at a crucial stage of development, could be expected to produce a dependency borne of frustration or deprivation *or* result in overindulgence on the part of the remaining parent or parent substitutes (in the case of loss of both parents). In turn, those experiencing frustration of dependency needs might be expected to seek a rewarding interpersonal relationship through marriage *or* be unable to obtain such a high level of need satisfaction through a heterosexual relationship, and therefore, choose not to commit themselves to a less gratifying relationship. Two possibilities derive from this assortment of alternatives: (1) the effects of parental loss on the alcohol dependent's relationship to marriage were differential and one cancelled out the other when analyzed; or (2) the effect of dependency needs may be of more importance in aspects of life other than marriage; early dependency needs contribute less heavily to the formation and maintenance of a marital relationship than do social skills acquired in childhood and adolescence.

If the setting at which various groups of alcohol dependents were studied is any indication of socioeconomic status and class value system, the skid-row alcohol dependent brings to the fore further problems. It has been shown that clinic and hospital groups evidence a larger proportion of men whose marriages are still intact. Moreover, these men tend to be younger. On the other hand, the homeless man on skid row has had less opportunity to acquire further social skills when he has not married; has possibly lost many acquired skills through simple disuse after having dissolved a marital relationship or has actively rejected the norms governing behavior after having lived on skid row. He is also considerably older.

The data show, for example, that half of the men who did marry have not lived within a marital situation for over ten years and many of these for over twenty. Thus, these men — who have inadequately learned, forgotten, or rejected the valuable social techniques acquired through marriage or through interaction within the mainstream of society — have the further problem of no family support when and if socialization or resocialization takes place.

Implications for Rehabilitation

Findings relating to the marital behavior of these alcohol dependents pose two problems in regard to rehabilitation. The first concerns priority. Where the allocation of finances and other resources are a factor and the feasibility of success must be considered, the married alcohol dependent or one who has been married is a better rehabilitation risk than the individual who never married. Since the married or formerly married alcohol dependent has demonstrated some capacity for close interpersonal relationships, there is a greater likelihood that he will be able to relate to rehabilitation personnel more adequately. Moreover, the alcohol dependent who is or has been married is generally more sophisticated in the use of decision-making techniques and social interaction skills both of which provide him with at least some basic equipment for negotiating within his social systems.

The second problem is that of motivating the homeless man, whether previously married or not, who lacks the support of concerned family members. The vast majority of the skid-row alcohol dependents in this study maintained minimal or no contact with their former spouse and family. A motivational substitute for family members, such as Synanon offers to drug dependents, could be offered, especially to the homeless alcohol dependents, in order to provide them with relatively constant and needed emotional support. For the married or recently separated alcohol dependent, the spouse must be involved as an integral part of the rehabilitation process, since she must be helped to understand her role in the pathology and to remain as a source of support and motivation. Her activities and the segments of her personality functioning which negate the client's progress require the help of rehabilitation professionals. In fact some of the group dynamics techniques (role playing, training in improved communication, etc.) suggested for the alcohol dependent could also be tried with the spouse. They would aid in clarifying problems and would also give her additional social skills training. The importance of working out with the wife her attitudes toward and responsibilities for her husband's drinking problem was documented by Clifford (1960).

7

Dependence upon Alcohol

For the rehabilitation of the alcohol dependent it is important to consider that not all individuals drink in the same way. Types of drinking and amounts differ. One of the purposes of this investigation was to shed light on the manner in which alcohol dependence developed and progressed. An understanding of the direction and intensity of drinking behavior can be most valuable to the practitioner in planning rehabilitation strategies.

If rehabilitation of the alcohol dependent is to succeed, there must be a pattern or sequence to steps taken in the rehabilitation process itself. Knowledge of drinking behavior in the individual and in the alcohol dependent group as a whole can be valuable in designing patterns of rehabilitation. These implications will be discussed in greater detail at the conclusion of this chapter.

Development of Alcohol Dependence

Level of alcohol dependence was defined in terms of both the frequency and intensity of drinking. Since dependence on alcohol either remained relatively constant over the years or at some point underwent marked change, the word "phase" was introduced to denote change. When no appreciable change in alcohol dependence was noted, the term "life phase" was used. If a marked change in alcohol dependence was noted which lasted over a period of years, the change was described as a "second phase." The previous level of dependence then became the initial, or first, phase. The frequency distributions of alcohol dependence according to phases is presented in Table 35.

Slightly over half the subjects were judged highly dependent on alcohol throughout their adult lives; an additional 24 percent became highly dependent during some later time in life. Before looking at some of the factors found to be related to alcohol dependence, let us turn briefly to initial experiences with alcohol.

Statistics have shown that, in societies where drinking is learned early, where the alcohol content of the drink is low, and where the

Table 35

Level of Alcohol Dependence

Alcohol Dependence	N	Percent
Life or Initial Phase		
Heavy	28	54.9
Moderate	17	33.3
Light	6	11.8
	51	
Continuation of Life Phase or Second Phase		
Heavy	44	83.0
Moderate	6	11.3
Light	3	5.7
	53	
Life or Initial and Second Phases		
Heavy-Heavier	6	11.8
Heavy-Heavy	22	43.1
Moderate-Heavy	12	23.5
Moderate-Moderate	5	9.8
Light-Moderate	1	2.0
Light-Light	3	5.9
Light-Heavy	2	3.9
	51	
Initial to Second Phase (Change)		
Increase	21	41.2
No change	30	58.8
Decrease	0	0.0
	51	
At Time of Interview		
Stable decrease to light	4	7.4
Stable decrease to moderate	2	3.7
Stable decrease to less heavy	1	1.8
	7	
Temporary decrease to light	12	22.2
Temporary decrease to moderate	1	1.8
Temporary decrease to less heavy	5	9.2
	18	
No change — still light	3	5.6
No change — still moderate	5	9.2
No change — still heavy	21	38.9
	54	

behavior is governed by specific norms, drinking is less likely to progress to pathologic dependence on alcohol. If early education in the correct use of alcohol is crucial, then serious efforts should be directed toward the problem of prevention.

The age at which drinking was initiated and continued with some regularity appeared to fall within the normative pattern of young male adult drinking behavior. Most began drinking at 18 or older (62 percent) and continued to drink (67 percent); the remainder, although experiencing alcohol at an earlier age, reported not drinking again until several years after their initial encounter. Although the group divided evenly as to the alcohol content contained in their first drink (high as in liquor, low as in beer and wine), slightly over half (54 percent) reported becoming intoxicated during their first drinking experience. This percentage would obviously increase if those whose first drink was taken with a meal in the home or for medicinal purposes were not taken into consideration. The relatively high proportion who became drunk on their first encounter with alcohol coupled with the fact that all subjects remembered the experience suggests the meaningfulness of the experience. Not only could the drinking experience be considered high in reward value in terms of effect, but, as Ullman (1953) pointed out, the fact that the memory of the experience remained intact suggests the importance attached to it.

Three-quarters of the alcohol dependents (74 percent) initially experienced alcohol outside of the home. These young men were more likely to have taken their first drink at a later age (Yates $\chi^2 = 664$, $df = 1$, $p < 0.01$), become intoxicated during their initial drinking experience (Fisher exact 2 = tailed = 0.05), and continued to drink with regularity (Yates $\chi^2 = 3.32$, $df = 1$, $p < 0.07$). Finally, subjects whose mothers did not drink at all were more likely to have taken their first drink among peer group members (Fisher exact 2 = tailed) = 0.03). Conflicting parental attitudes toward the use of alcohol or concern with establishing masculinity with their peers might have initially motivated these individuals to experiment with alcohol outside the family environment.

Comparison of these data to those obtained by other investigators, both inside and outside the United States, illustrates cross-cultural differences in drinking behavior. For example, across three studies conducted in Italy, France, and Switzerland an average of 70 percent of the subjects interviewed reported having experienced at least the initial contact with alcoholic beverages prior to age 16 (Lolli, et al., 1958; Sadoun and Lolli, 1962; Devrient and Lolli, 1962). In contrast, across four studies conducted within this country an average of only one-quarter reported having consumed alcohol prior to this age (Feeney, et al., 1955; Ulman, 1953; Selzer and Holloway, 1957; Lolli et al., 1960).

Similarly, in other countries (Lolli, et al., 1958; Sadoun and Lolli, 1962; Devrient and Lolli, 1962), a greater percentage reported having consumed wine or beer as their first drink; whereas, in this country, a greater percentage reported consuming hard liquor (Ulman, 1953; Terry et al., 1957; Lolli et al., 1960). Moreover, the extent to which the first drink was consumed within the home environment or in connection with a specific social event was greater in studies done outside the U.S.A. and indicates that drinking under such circumstances is sanctioned in a formal way by family, religious, and social custom.

Returning to factors associated with alcohol dependence, the data indicate that subjects rated as heavy drinkers during their first or life phase of drinking and as "not changed" on their second drinking phase, dependence on alcohol was found not to be associated with specific stress or life problems but must have been associated instead with a dependency which evolved earlier in life (Fisher exact (2 = tail) = 0.001; Yates χ^2 = 9.601, df = 1, $p < 0.002$). On the other hand, the originally light to moderate drinkers became heavy drinkers only after or concurrent with problem or crisis situations. The implication is that some of these alcohol dependents were able to function adequately without recourse to alcohol to a point — the remainder were not able to cope with life even without specific problems posing a threat to themselves or their way of life.

This phenomenon would indicate that while life stress serves to increase or exacerbate dependency on alcohol, for many drinkers the dependency on alcohol arises early in life and is associated with psycho- and sociodynamic conditions which begin early and extend over time. This thesis is partially corroborated by the finding that drinkers with early unstable family relationships tended to maintain the same level of drinking throughout most of their lives. On the other hand, subjects who had not experienced the loss of one or more parents through death, divorce, or separation tended to show an increase in level of drinking during their later adult years. Level of intensity of alcohol dependency is not involved in this finding, only change in intensity. This relationship is presented in Table 36.

The tendency toward heavier drinking was observed among those with an eighth-grade education or less (Table 37). This might indicate that longer periods in school allowed for the development of better social skills, which enabled subjects to negotiate life's problems with

Table 36

**Relationship Between Change from
First to Second Phase of Alcohol
Dependence and Parental Loss**

| | Change | | |
Parental Loss	Increase	No Change	Total
No	15	11	26
Yes	7	17	24
	22	28	50

Yates χ^2 = 3,045, df = 1, $p < 0.081$

Table 37

**Relationship Between the Subject's
Education and Initial or Life Phase of
Alcohol Dependence**

| | Alcohol Dependence | | |
Education	Heavy	Light-Medium	Total
Grammar school or less	14	3	17
High school and beyond	12	18	30
	26	21	47

χ^2 = 7.87, df = 1, $p < 0.01$

less dependence on alcohol. Similarly, those whose first or life phase dependence upon alcohol was high were less likely to have participated in outside activities during their youth. The early inability to or lack of opportunity for relating meaningfully in individual or group relationships may have predisposed these subjects to later difficulty in forming interpersonal relationships. This association is presented in Table 38, (χ^2 = 10.17, df = 1, p 0.01).

Factors found to be associated with alcohol dependence indicate that the rehabilitation process must proceed on two levels concurrently. On the "here and now" reality level, the client must be helped to cope with existing life situations and even sheltered from

Table 38

**Relationship Between First or Life
Phase of Alcohol Dependence and
Activities as Youth**

| | | Alcohol Dependence | |
Activities	Heavy	Light-Medium	Total
Zero to One	14	2	16
Two or More	12	19	31
	26	21	47

$$\chi^2 = 10.17, \quad df = 1, \quad p < 0.01$$

overstressful pressures early in his rehabilitation. In other words, the environmental manipulation component is most important in re-habilitating the alcohol dependent. However, in addition to helping him cope with the "here and now," counseling must also enable the alcohol dependent to face and deal with the earlier emotional landmarks in his life, such as emotional loss and social deprivation, which have left their continuing impact upon his personality functioning.

Motivation for Rehabilitation

One major area with which the rehabilitation professional must concern himself is the alcohol dependent's perception of his problem and his motivation for treatment. The frequency and percent distributions showing the way in which the alcohol dependent perceives himself and his problem are presented in Table 39. Although 82 percent were judged to be highly dependent on alcohol only one-third admitted this dependence by labeling themselves alcoholic. Since recognition of the problem is a necessary step toward rehabilitation, such denial poses a real barrier to rehabili-tation and a challenge to the rehabilitation professional who attempts to help him. In this instance one might call into question the use of the voluntary self-determinative philosophy which has for so long been a major philosophical tenet of most psychologically oriented treatment. Perhaps more directive, aggressive, outreach

Table 39

**Perception of Self and of the Problem
by the Alcohol Dependent**

Perception	N	Percent
The Problem		
Difference Between Alcohol Dependent and Nonalcohol Dependent?		
Control	8	18.6
Need	19	44.2
Severity	6	14.0
Control and need	2	4.6
Control and severity	2	4.6
Need and severity	2	4.6
Other	4	9.3
	43	
Can Alcohol Dependents Be "Cured" or Stop Drinking?		
Yes	34	73.9
No	12	26.1
	46	
The Self		
Did Subject Admit to His Dependence on Alcohol?		
Yes	17	32.1
No	37	67.9
	53	
Is Drinking Problem-Associated?		
Is problem-associated	14	40.0
Is not problem-associated	5	14.3
Was progressively worse from the start	16	45.7
	35	

treatment techniques are indicated in the case of the alcohol dependent, even the use of authority in a helpful manner. The findings show that such treatment approaches merit further testing in that those alcohol dependents who accepted any sort of treatment for their problems were those whose antisocial behavior compelled society's attention in the form of such treatment.

The frequency and percent distributions for number of arrests as a result of public intoxication are presented in Table 40. As shown,

98

Table 40

Arrests for Public Intoxication

Number of Arrests	N	Percent
Never	12	24.0
1-3 times	11	22.0
4-10 times	15	30.0
More than 10 times	12	24.0
	50	

Table 41

Relationship Between Times Arrested for Drinking and Times Attended AA

AA Attendance	Arrests		
	1 to over 17	Never	Total
Attended	18	4	22
Never attended	4	7	11
Total	22	11	33

Yates χ^2 = 4.94, df = 1, $p < 0.05$

Table 42

Relationship Between Times Arrested for Drinking and Times Hospitalized for Alcohol Dependence

Hospitalized	Arrested		
	Yes	No	Total
Yes	18	1	19
No	15	10	25
Total	33	11	44

Yates χ^2 = 5.21, df = 1, $p < 0.05$

one-quarter reported having never been arrested for drinking; one-quarter, an excessive number of times; and the half remaining, under ten times. The data show that subjects who reported never having been arrested also reported never having attended AA or been hospitalized for alcoholic treatment. These relationships are presented in Tables 41 and 42, respectively.

The need for some external authority source to help the alcohol dependent recognize his dependence upon alcohol is further reinforced by the finding that subjects who reported having been arrested for public intoxication tended to have been the ones who admitted their dependence on alcohol. This relationship is presented in Table 43. Again, the severity of the drinking problem is recognized in terms of society's definition of wrongful behavior.

The frequency and percent distributions for questions pertaining to the motivation of the alcohol dependent in regard to eliminating his reliance on the "bottle" may be seen in Table 44. Denial of dependency is again evidenced by those who claimed not to have a serious drinking problem or to be already "cured." Nearly a third wished to stop drinking, while another third expressed satisfaction with their current status. A very few felt that they could not stop even if they wanted to. Most reported having tried to stop drinking at least one time in their life, but few met with significant success.

In the area of motivation, attention is drawn to the finding that alcohol dependents who expressed the desire to stop drinking were more often those between 40 and 49 years of age or 60 years and older (Table 45). One conclusion that might be drawn from this finding is that younger men (under 40) either cannot admit to or do not recognize the seriousness of their dependency upon alcohol. For the rehabilitation practitioner this indicates the necessity of increased focus on definition of the problem within the counseling framework when working with younger alcohol dependents. The reason for the lack of desire to stop drinking in men between 50 and 60 years of age could be that, although they might admit their dependence on alcohol, its threat to their health is not as real as it is to those who are older.

As indicated by Table 46, the problem of getting the alcohol dependent into some form of treatment is formidable indeed. Over half the subjects reported never having been admitted to any type of treatment. When this figure is combined with the 21.7 percent who were admitted only once, four-fifths of the population can be described as having had minimal formalized treatment.

These findings are understandable within the framework of the underdeveloped-social-skills hypothesis. Since many of the alcohol dependents reported having had relatively little in the way of

Table 43

Relationship Between Times Arrested for Drinking and Admission of Alcohol Dependence

Admit Dependence	0-10	Arrests Over 17	Total
Yes	10	16	26
No	27	6	33
Total	37	22	59

Yates $\chi^2 = 3.34$, $df = 1$, $p < 0.08$

Table 44

Motivation to Reduce Alcohol Dependence

Orientation Toward Reduced Dependence	N	Percent
Did Subject Wish to Be "Cured" or Stop Drinking?		
Yes	15	32.6
No	14	30.4
No, drinking not serious enough	9	19.6
Already "cured"	4	8.7
Doubts could (defeatist attitude)	4	8.7
	46	
Could Subject Stop Drinking If He Wanted to?		
Yes	18	69.2
Yes on condition	4	15.4
No	4	15.4
	26	

Table 44 *(continued)*

How Many Times Did Subject Try to Stop Drinking?	*N*	*Percent*
Never	9	18.0
Once	12	24.0
2-7 times; several	19	38.0
Infinite, repeatedly	10	20.0
	50	

Total Period Subject Stopped Drinking		
Weeks	8	22.2
Months	11	30.6
Years	17	47.2
	36	

Motivation to Stop Drinking		
Internal (self primarily responsible)	12	41.4
External	10	34.5
Combination internal and external (no agencies involved)	4	13.8
Combination internal and external (no agencies involved)	3	10.3
	29	

Table 45

Relationship Between the Subject's Age and His Desire to Stop Drinking

	Had Desire to Stop Drinking		
Age	*Yes*	*No or Doubt*	*Total*
Under 40, or 50-59	4	12	16
40-49 or 60 and over	11	6	17
Total	15	18	33

$$x^2 = 5.24, df = 1, p \leqslant 0.05$$

Table 46

Admissions for Alcoholic Treatment

Admissions	N	Percent
Number		
Never	27	58.7
Once	10	21.7
Two-three	5	10.9
More than three	4	8.7
	46	
Type of Admitting Institution		
Correctional (nonvoluntary)	6	31.6
VA, general, or state hospital (voluntary)	6	31.6
Rehabilitation Facility (voluntary)	2	10.5
Correctional and rehabilitation facility	1	5.3
VA, general, or state hospital and rehabilitation facility	3	15.8
Correctional and VA, general, or state hospital	1	5.3
	19	
Total Length of Stays		
One month	3	17.6
Two-three months	4	23.5
Four-six months	7	41.2
Over six months	3	17.6
	17	
Time of Year Admitted		
Fall	1	16.7
Winter	5	83.3
Spring	0	0
Summer	0	0
	6	

activities outside the home during early personality development, their reluctance to participate in the social negotiations required to take part effectively in socially institutionalized types of treatment is understandable. One might also speculate that such underdeveloped social skills engender an avoidance of the authority structure which formalized treatment implies.

As shown in Table 47 four-fifths of the population attended at least one AA meeting. One-third of those who attended AA did so for a period fo six months or less; one-fourth attended AA for five

Table 47

Involvement in Alcoholics Anonymous (AA)

Attendance and Attitude	N	Percent
Attended AA		
Yes	44	80.0
No	11	20.0
	55	
Circumstance of Initial Attendance		
Attended with a friend	11	34.4
Attended alone	2	6.2
Friend suggested	4	12.5
Attended on own	7	21.9
Attendance required	2	6.2
By chance	3	9.4
Nothing better to do	3	9.4
	32	
Number Times Attended		
1	1	4.0
2-10	14	56.0
11-25	2	8.0
Over 25	8	32.0
	25	
Total Period Attended		
Less than 1 month	1	4.4
1-6 months	7	30.4
Over 6 months to 1 year	3	13.0
Over 1 year to 5 years	6	26.1
Over 5 years	6	26.1
	23	
When Attended		
Within past year or at present	8	34.8
Within past 5 years	11	47.8
More than 5 years ago	4	17.4
	23	
Helped by AA		
Helped by	9	22.0
Not helped	32	78.0
	41	
Feelings Toward AA		
Liked or positive attitude	14	38.9
Disliked or negative attitude	16	44.4
Ambivalent attitude	6	16.7
	36	

years or more. Although 40 percent expressed some positive feelings toward AA, 80 percent of those who attended felt they received no help.

One of the major reasons that 44 percent of the alcohol dependent subjects in this study reported totally negative feelings toward Alcoholics Anonymous might have been due to their inability to tolerate the confrontation of the members concerning their alcohol dependent behavior. This hypothesis receives some support from the findings that those alcohol dependents who had positive attitudes toward Alcoholics Anonymous and who felt helped by this group-encounter-like experience were those with lower socioeconomic backgrounds (Yates $\chi^2 = 3.89, df = 1, p < 0.05$). They may have been more accustomed to being confronted with more dogmatic, direct, and maybe even harsh discipline in their families. Although Alcoholics Anonymous offers emotional support there is an element of confrontation built into the group process.

Summary

Dependence on alcohol was discussed in terms of four areas of development: (1) initial experience with alcoholic beverages, (2) subsequent dependency on alcohol, (3) consequent social and antisocial behavior, and (4) motivational factors in reducing this dependency. In turn, variables specific to these areas have been related to prior levels of adjustment.

The data indicate that initial drinking generally was not tied to family or religious custom but, rather, learned outside the home and without specific norms to guide its regulation. Eighty-two percent of the skid rowers were classified as highly dependent on alcohol, with 55 percent judged highly dependent since early adulthood. Alcohol dependence among the 55 percent appeared not to have been crisis-precipitated but, rather, stemmed from something which occurred or did not occur much earlier in life. The heavier drinkers tended to have come from broken homes, to have participated minimally in activities outside the home, and to have received less formal education. These factors point to the development of dependent behavior as a partial result of prior deficiencies in interpersonal relationships and lack of social skills, the tools needed to successfully negotiate within social systems.

Institutional affiliations reported by most of the men were

generally poor. Although 80 percent had attended AA, the majority did so relatively few times and over a short period of time. Over three-quarters expressed the attitude that AA was of little or no benefit to them, and the majority expressed negative attitudes toward the organization itself. Further, less than half reported ever having received treatment for their alcoholic problem. Of those, one-third were committed involuntarily as a result of excessive arrests. Those arrested for public intoxication were able to admit their dependence on alcohol and reported AA attendance and admissions for alcoholic treatment. These findings suggest the value of what has been referred to as constructive coercion.

Implications for Rehabilitation

It is valuable to note that not all subjects in the skid-row alcohol dependent population drank heavily throughout their lives. There were periods in the lives of these men when they were successful in reducing their drinking and even abstaining. This would suggest that successful rehabilitation is possible if it can be determined what factors contribute to the reduction of drinking.

The importance of dealing with psychological factors in planning the rehabilitation of the alcohol dependent is confirmed by the data concerning drinking behavior. While the authors do not rule out physiological causes of alcohol dependency, the fact that serious alcohol dependents are capable of controlling their drinking when adequately motivated adds weight to the importance of psychodynamic and social factors.

The fact that the alcohol dependent subjects who came from unstable family environments maintained a constant level of drinking throughout their lives would indicate the importance of continued stressful situations in contributing to dependence upon alcohol. This would suggest the value of working with the alcohol dependent in a psychosocial milieu which is stress free at least in the initial phases of rehabilitation. Coping with psychosocial problems is a necessary part of the rehabilitation of the alcohol dependent but should be brought on by the rehabilitation therapist gradually in a controlled manner at a later point in the rehabilitation process.

The findings of this study corroborate the well-known information concerning the great difficulty encountered in getting the alcohol dependent to accept rehabilitation treatment. Those alcohol dependents who had received treatment (hospitalization, AA, etc.) were essentially those who had been guilty of antisocial behavior and arrested. In other words, it was the response of society to their antisocial behavior which precipitated or compelled the acceptance of treatment. This finding indicates consideration of the need for a directive approach to the alcohol dependent when offering rehabilitation services. In other words, in the case of the confirmed alcohol dependent there should be some experimentation with programs that involve what might be called aggressive rehabilitation. These programs would in some ways parallel the aggressive social casework with the hard-core or multiproblem family.

For the most part, the field of rehabilitation has in the past offered services on a self-determinative basis. The client was required to seek and apply for the rehabilitation services he felt were needed. If the client who is highly dependent upon alcohol does not have the ego strength to apply and negotiate through the complex intake processes of the conventional rehabilitation agency, perhaps the rehabilitation agency should adopt a persistent outreach philosophy in taking rehabilitation services to the client. The value of experimenting with an aggressive rehabilitation method for helping the alcohol dependent is further reinforced by the finding that 75 percent of our subjects expressed optimism concerning the probability that alcohol dependency could be "cured." With an aggressive extension of rehabilitation treatment to the alcohol dependent, perhaps such optimism, though not always real, can serve as a starting point for motivating the client.

8

Vocational Behavior of the Alcohol Dependent

The vocational activities of the individual in our society constitute a substantial part of his life. Not only is the major portion of his waking hours occupied by work, but his social status, his feelings of security, and his perception of self-adequacy are influenced by it. It is rare when two people meet for the first time that they do not ask each other "what they do," their vocation. In a sense, people adjust their relationship to one another on the basis of work. The social value of productivity in our culture is strong indeed.

Thus, information was sought concerning the vocational behavior of the alcohol dependent subjects. For, if rehabilitation of the alcohol dependent is to be successful, feelings of vocational adequacy are absolutely essential for the client. In order to attempt selective vocational placement for the alcohol dependent, awareness of past vocational adjustment patterns is necessary.

The finding which stands out in this study is that, for the most part, alcohol dependents evidence a fairly substantial measure of vocational productivity from the standpoints of longevity and level of attainment. The vocational performance of the subjects leaves one with a feeling of guarded optimism concerning rehabilitation potential. A number of subjects took great pride in their work and, in some cases, loss of their vocation took the form of an emotional loss, quite like the loss of a human love object.

Initial Work Experience

Presented in Table 48 are the response distributions for questions related to the first job experience. For many, the time was the Depression. One-third were 14 years old or younger at the time of their first job. Over half worked while going to school. Nearly two-thirds of first jobs were full-time. Roughly three-quarters of the jobs were at the semiskilled and unskilled levels. Over one-third of first jobs fell within the "clerical, sales" category and consisted primarily of delivery work. Nearly one-fifth involved the food industry ("service" category) where the men worked as waiters,

Table 48

Initial Work Experience

First Job	N	Percent
Age		
Under 15	16	33.3
15 and over	32	66.7
	48	
Full- or Part-Time		
Part-time	9	17.6
Full-time	32	62.8
Seasonal	2	3.9
Seasonal/summer/part-time	3	5.9
Summers/vacations	5	9.8
	51	
Education		
Completed	23	43.4
Not completed	30	56.6
	53	
Occupational Category		
Professional, managerial, technical	0	0.0
Clerical Sales	19	38.8
Service	9	18.4
Farm, fishing, forestry, etc.	6	12.2
Processing	2	4.1
Machine trades	1	2.0
Bench work	2	4.1
Structural work	8	16.3
Miscellaneous	2	4.1
	49	
Skill Level		
Skilled	14	29.2
Semiskilled	10	20.8
Unskilled	15	31.2
Sales	9	18.8
	48	

busboys, and cook's helpers. Another 16 percent involved the "structural work" field.

Of great importance to the vocational development of any individual is his first exposure to the world of work, particularly the type of job and his adjustment to it in terms of his own feelings of adequacy and security. Those alcohol dependents whose education was complete (never returned to school) were more likely to have worked full-time at their first job; and, in turn, those who worked full-time were more likely to have worked at a skilled job or better. These relationships are presented in Tables 49 and 50. These young men, then, although taking an important step toward independence, whether forced or not, brought with them certain job competencies. On the other hand, those whose first job was part-time encountered the world of work with little in the way of job skill but, at the same time, were not taking a major step toward independence — they still had the security that comes with remaining in school and not having total vocational responsibility.

Table 49

Relationship Between First Job Part-Time or Full-time and Education Completed

		First Job	
Education	*Part-Time*	*Full-Time*	*Total*
Not completed	16	5	21
Completed	3	25	28
Total	19	30	49

Yates $\chi^2 = 19.000$, $df = 1$, $p < 0.000$

Table 50

**Relationship Between First Job
Part-Time or Full-Time and Job
Skill**

Job	Skilled or Better	Job Skill Semi- or Unskilled	Total
Part-time	1	15	16
Full-time	12	18	30
Total	13	33	46

Yates χ^2 = 4.316, df = 1, $p < 0.038$

Subjects no longer in school at the time of their first job were those whose fathers favored a child other than the subject and were those whose mothers were perceived as the authority figure (decisionmaker) within the home. Mothers of these subjects either favored the subject or favored someone other than the subject. The perceived display of favoritism by the mother, then, whatever the object, was significantly more common among subjects who worked and did not or were not able to assume a dependent position of being a student and a child within the home (see Tables 51, 52, and 53).

Subjects who began working at age 14 or under not only entered the world of work at an early age but they also were more likely to have experienced parental loss than were those who began working at a later age (Table 54). Many, then, had to assume, in addition to responsibilities of the job itself, some of the financial responsibilities of an absent male head of household. Again, subjects who began working at age 14 or under came significantly more often from homes in which the mother was the authority figure (decisionmaker). This relationship is presented in Table 55.

Thus, in the case of the alcohol dependent compelled to enter the world of work at the age of 14 years or under, this very fact may have contributed to his need for dependency. For the ten subjects who came from homes in which the mother was dominant and in which they might have partially filled the role of an absent father (emotional as well as financial) incestuous fantasies with accom-

Table 51

Relationship Between Education
Completed at First Job and Fathers
Favorite Child

	Education Completed		
Father's Favorite	No	Yes	Total
No favorite	9	0	9
Not subject	1	5	6
Total	10	5	15

Fisher exact (2-tail) =0.004

Table 52

Relationship Between Education
Completed at First Job and Perceived
Authority Figure

	Education Completed		
Decision Maker	No	Yes	Total
Mother	5	15	20
Father or shared	14	2	16
Total	19	17	36

$\chi^2 = 3.88$, $df=1$, $p < 0.05$

panying guilt as well as deep hostility toward the mother may have been aroused. Such subjects may have turned to alcohol to reduce or avoid the frustrations and tensions which arouse from such unconscious conflicts. In such cases rehabilitation would best involve situations in which the subject could experience a reeducation in his relationship with women.

Table 53

**Relationship Between Education
Completed at First Job and Mother's
Favorite Child**

	Education Completed		
Mother's Favorite	No	Yes	Total
No favorite	9	0	9
Subject or other favorite	2	14	16
Total	11	14	25

Yates χ^2=14.52, df=1, p<0.001

Table 54

**Relationship Between Age at First Job
and Parental Loss**

	Age at First Job		
Parental Loss	Under 15	15 and Over	Total
No	5	20	25
Yes	10	11	21
Total	15	31	46

Yates χ^2=2.805, df=1, p<0.094

Table 55

**Relationship Between Age at First Job
and Perceived Authority Figure**

	Age at First Job		
Decision Maker	Under 15	15 and Over	Total
Mother	10	9	19
Father	3	21	24
Total	13	30	43

χ^2=8.07, df=1, p<0.01

The extent to which subjects sought help such as AA was reflected by certain indicators of a more stable and lengthy socialization process as youths. Specifically, AA attendance of more than ten times and over one year in total time tended to be related to being age 15 and over at the time of the first job and to having been in school at the time of the first job, respectively. Finally, subjects no longer in school at the time of their first job were more likely as adults to have been arrested for public intoxication. These relationships are presented in Tables 56, 57, and 58. Not only was their childhood longer but the transition between adolescence and adulthood as reflected by working was less abrupt.

Table 56

Relationship Between Age at First Job and AA Attendance

	Age at First Job		
Times Attended AA	*Under 15*	*Over 15*	*Total*
10 and under	6	7	13
11 and over	0	8	8
Total	6	15	21

Fisher exact (2=tail) =0.064

Table 57

Relationship Between Education Completed at First Job and Total Length of AA Attendance

	Education Completed		
Length of AA Attendance	*No*	*Yes*	*Total*
1 year maximum	2	9	13
Over 1 year	8	4	8
Total	10	13	23

Fisher exact (2=tail) =0.052

Table 58

**Relationship Between Education
Completed at First Job and Times
Arrested for Drinking**

	Education Completed		
Times Arrested	No	Yes	Total
1-17	12	24	36
Never	8	4	12
Total	20	28	48

$\chi^2 = 4.12$, $df=1$, $p < 0.05$

What is most important for the field of vocational rehabilitation is that those alcohol dependents whose first job entailed little in the way of job competency drank heavily initially or throughout their lives and evidenced no change in alcohol dependence; nor did their heavy drinking seem to be associated with or precipitated by specific crisis situations. These relationships are presented in Tables 59, 60, and 61. This suggests that, in general, these men brought little in the way of vocational competencies to their adult life and compensated by drinking for the lack of psychosocial satisfaction through meaningful work. Moreover, it is possible that these subjects drank for peer-group acceptance in a vocational milieu where drinking was very common.

Table 59

**Relationship Between First Job Skill
and First or Life Phase of Alcohol
Dependence**

Alcohol Dependence in First or Life Phase	First Job Skill		
	Skilled or Better	Semi- or Unskilled	Total
Heavy	3	23	26
Light-medium	10	9	19
Total	13	32	45

Yates $\chi^2 = 7.134$, $df = 1$, $p < 0.008$

Table 60

**Relationship Between First Job Skill
and Change from First to Second Phase
of Alcohol Dependence**

| | First Job Skill | | |
Change in Drinking Pattern	Skilled or Better	Semi- or Unskilled	Total
Increase	9	10	19
No change	4	21	25
Total	13	31	44

Yates χ^2 = 3.707, df = 1, $p <$ 0.054

Table 61

**Relationship Between First Job Skill
and Problem-Associated Drinking**

| | First Job Skill | | |
Drinking was Problem-Associated	Skilled or Better	Semi- or Unskilled	Total
No	2	17	19
Yes	6	5	11
Total	8	22	30

Fisher exact (2-tail) = 0.030

These findings tend to place emphasis on the importance of selective vocational placement in the rehabilitation of the alcohol dependent client. As much as possible, within the capabilities and potential of the individual, jobs must be sufficiently challenging and carry some degree of status. This is important because the major life problem of these individuals appears to be centered around feelings of inadequacy and the inability to carry out adequate social negotiations. Menial occupations just for the sake of expediency of placements, unless they can meet the above criteria, should be avoided by the rehabilitating agency.

General Vocational History

Table 62 summarizes the alcohol dependent's employment history. The number of full-time jobs ranged from one to more than eight and averaged between three and four with the median falling at three. The number of occupational categories involved ranged from

Table 62

General Vocational History

Full-Time Jobs	N	Percent
Number Held		
1	5	9.1
2	12	21.8
3	12	21.8
4	8	14.6
5	10	18.2
6	4	7.3
7	1	1.8
8 or more	3	5.4
	55	
Period Longest-Held		
1-2 years	1	1.9
3-5 years	7	13.2
6.10 years	10	18.9
11-15 years	8	15.1
16-20 years	6	11.3
21-life	21	39.6
	53	
Skill Level of Longest-Held		
Professional, managerial	4	8.2
Technical	0	0.0
Skilled	23	46.9
Semiskilled	16	32.6
Unskilled	4	8.2
Semi- or unskilled	1	2.0
Sales	1	2.0
	49	

Table 62 (*continued*)

Full-Time Jobs	*N*	*Percent*
Highest Skill Level		
Professional, managerial	5	9.1
Technical	1	1.8
Skilled	30	54.6
Semiskilled	16	29.1
Unskilled	3	5.4
	55	
Number of Job Categories		
1	8	14.6
2	24	43.6
3	14	25.4
4	5	9.1
5	4	7.3
	55	
Category of Longest-Held		
Professional, technical, managerial	4	7.5
Clerical, sales	7	13.2
Service	14	26.4
Farm, fishing, forestry, etc.	2	3.8
Processing	4	7.5
Machine trades	1	1.9
Bench work	0	0.0
Structural work	16	30.2
Miscellaneous	5	9.4
	53	

one to five and averaged between two and three with the median occurring at two. The median skill level for both the longest-held full-time job and for the highest skill level achieved was "skilled". For 30 percent the category of the longest-held job was "structural work," for one-quarter "service," and for one-fifth either "professional managerial" or "clerical sales."

As might be expected, subjects whose home environment was unstable (parental loss through death or divorce) were less occupationally and vocationally stable (more change), in terms of both the number of full-time jobs and the number of vocational categories in which jobs were held, than were subjects who did not come from broken homes. When loss of a parent did occur, vocational stability was poorer when the loss took place after the subject's twelfth birthday. However, those who lost a parent prior to age 6 tended to have achieved a lesser degree of job competency than did those who experienced loss later than age 5. These relationships are presented in Tables 63, 64, 65, and 66.

Table 63

Relationship Between Number of Full-
Time Jobs and Parental Loss

		Number Full-Time Jobs	
Parental Loss	1-2	3 and over	Total
No	13	15	28
Yes	4	21	25
Total	17	36	53

$$\chi^2 = 5.62, df = 1, p < 0.02$$

Table 64

Relationship Between Number of Occupational Categories of Full-Time Jobs
and Parental Loss

		Number of Categories	
Parental Loss	1-2	3 and over	Total
No	22	9	31
Yes	8	14	22
Total	30	23	53

$$\text{Yates } \chi^2 = 4.943, df = 1, p < 0.026$$

Table 65

Relationship Between Number of Occupational Categories of Full-Time Jobs
and Age of Subject at Parental Loss

| | Number of Categories | | |
Age at Parental Loss	1-2	3 and over	Total
0-12	11	8	19
13-17	0	6	6
Total	11	14	25

Yates χ^2 = 4.06, df = 1, $p < 0.05$

Table 66

Relationship Between Highest Skill
Level of Full-Time Jobs and Age at
Parental Loss

| | Highest Skill Level | | |
Age at Parental Loss	Skilled or Better	Semi- or Unskilled	Total
0-5	2	5	7
6-17	12	3	15
Total	14	8	22

Yates χ^2 = 3.46, df = 1, $p < 0.07$

In addition, early parental loss influenced present motivation to seek work, an important variable in rehabilitation. Those subjects who were no longer looking for work were more likely to have experienced early parental loss (Yates χ^2 = 6.683, df = 1, $p < 0.05$) and to have been less occupationally stable in terms of a greater number of job changes (χ^2 = 4.36, df = 1, $p < 0.05$).

Paradoxically, those subjects who reported the greatest and least opportunity for social experiences in their growth attained the lower skill levels in their adulthood, while those with moderate amounts of social experience achieved higher vocational skill levels (Tables 67 and 68).

Table 67

**Relationship Between Highest Skill
Level of All Full-Time Jobs and Activities as a Youth**

| Number of Activities | Highest Skill Level | | |
	Skilled or Better	Semi- or Unskilled	Total
0, 1, 4 or more	13	16	37
2-3	19	2	21
Total	32	18	50

$$\chi^2 = 4.52, df = 1, p < 0.05$$

Table 68

**Relationship Between Skill of Longest-
Held Full-Time Job and Activities as a
Youth**

| Number of Activities | Skill of Longest Full-Time Job | | |
	Skilled or Better	Semi- or Unskilled	Total
0, 1, 4 or more	9	15	24
2-3	16	5	21
	25	20	45

$$\chi^2 = 6.790, df = 1, p < 0.01$$

Lack of consistent vocational performance was related to dependency on alcohol. Individuals who were the heavier drinkers from the start were more likely to have made more job changes both in terms of number of full-time jobs held and number of various job categories worked in. In addition, lower skill level in job attainment was more likely to have occurred for heavier drinkers and where drinking was not associated with life problems (Tables 69, 70, 71, and 72).

Table 69

Relationship Between Number of Full-Time Jobs and First Phase of Alcohol Dependence

Alcohol Dependence in First Phase	Number of Full-Time Jobs 1-4	5 and over	Total
Heavy	16	12	28
Light-moderate	20	3	23
Total	36	15	51

$$\chi^2 = 5.40, \, df = 1, \, p < 0.05$$

Table 70

Relationship Between Number of Occupational Categories of Full-Time Jobs and First Phase of Alcohol Dependence

Alcohol Dependence in First Phase	Number of Occupational Categories 1-2	3 and over	Total
Heavy	13	15	28
Light-moderate	18	5	23
Total	31	20	51

$$\text{Yates } \chi^2 = 4.115, \, df = 1, \, p < 0.043$$

Table 71

**Relationship Between Highest Skill
Level of All Full-Time Jobs and First
Phase of Alcohol Dependence**

Alcohol Dependence in First Phase	Highest Skill Level		
	Skilled or Better	Semi- or Unskilled	Total
Heavy	14	14	28
Light-moderate	20	3	23
Total	34	17	51

Yates χ^2 = 6.187, df = 1, $p < 0.013$

Table 72

**Relationship Between Highest Skill
Level of All Full-Time Jobs and
Problem-Associated Drinking**

Problem-Associated Drinking	Highest Skill Level		
	Skilled or Better	Semi- or Unskilled	Total
No	10	11	21
Yes	12	2	14
Total	22	13	35

Yates χ^2 = 3.717, df = 1, $p < 0.054$

Those subjects of lower socioeconomic status were more likely to have felt positively toward AA as a helping agency. They also were slightly more likely to have experienced more arrests, which may have been a motivating factor in their maintaining a relationship with AA (Tables 73, 74, and 75).

Table 73

**Relationship Between Skill of Longest-
Held Full-Time Job and Feelings
Toward AA**

| Feelings Toward AA | Skill of Longest-Held Full-Time Job | | Total |
	Skilled or Better	Semi- or Unskilled	
Positive	4	9	13
Not positive	15	4	19
Total	19	13	32

Yates χ^2 = 5.565, df = 1, $p < 0.018$

Table 74

**Relationship Between Skill of Longest-
Held Full-Time Job and Help from AA**

| Help from AA | Skill Longest-Held Full-Time Job | | Total |
	Skilled or Better	Semi- or Unskilled	
Yes	2	6	8
No	19	9	28
Total	21	15	36

Fisher exact (2-tail) = 0.078

Table 75

**Relationship Between Skill of Longest-
Held Full-Time Job and Times Arrested
for Public Intoxication**

| Number of Arrests | Skill of Longest-Held Full-Time Job | | Total |
	Skilled or Better	Semi- or Unskilled	
0-17	20	13	33
Over 17	3	8	11
Total	23	21	44

χ^2 = 3.67, df = 1, $p < 0.10$

Final Work Experiences

Tables 76 and 77 indicate characteristics of last job experiences and last full-time job experiences of the research population. Last jobs which were categorized within the "service" occupations and which were full time (as opposed to part time or daily) were more often held by subjects who expressed a positive attitude toward school and participated moderately in boyhood activities (Tables 78 and 79). The ability to relate to others in a positive way and with some degree of success as a youth appears to be related to present employment success, even though limited, and again indicates the importance of helping the alcohol dependent develop social skills during the rehabilitation process.

Although, in general, the frequency tables suggest a lowering of group skills from initial work experiences to present work experiences, the common belief that alcohol dependents go downhill in all aspects of life may not be totally valid — it appears not to hold true for vocational skill level. When last and last full-time jobs were of a skilled level or better, the longest-held full-time job was skilled or better and the highest skill level achieved was skilled or better (Yates $\chi^2 = 10.485$, $df = 1$, $p < 0.001$; Yates $\chi^2 = 14.51$, $df = 1$, $p < 0.001$; Yates $\chi^2 = 6.822$, $df = 1$, $p < 0.009$; Yates $\chi^2 = 12.7$, $df = 1$, $p < 0.001$). From a rehabilitation standpoint this finding is of notable significance, because if vocational skill does not deteriorate rapidly in the alcohol dependent, higher levels of placement are possible and can serve to motivate the client.

Even in the case of last jobs, skill level was related to phases of alcohol dependence. Those subjects whose last jobs were at the lower skill levels were more likely to have been the heavier drinkers throughout their adulthood. It is difficult to determine whether drinking influenced skill attainment or boredom on the job exacerbated drinking (Tables 80 and 81).

Motivation can be a dynamic factor in helping the alcohol dependent reduce his dependence upon alcohol. The factors involved in the research population's present motivation to work, although already detailed in earlier tables, are outlined again in Table 82. It is difficult to know how truthful subjects were in their statements concerning their desire to work since social desirability may have influenced their responses.

The rehabilitation worker must realistically confront the seriousness of the problem of motivating the alcohol dependent to work regularly. The vast majority of men were not employed at the time of the interview; some of these reported occasional daily work once

Table 76

Last Job Experience

Last Job	N	Percent
Part- or Full-Time		
Part-time	2	3.8
Full-time	16	30.2
Seasonal	4	7.5
Daily	19	35.8
Part time or daily	12	22.6
	53	
Duration		
Under 6 months	10	21.3
6 months to under 1 year	4	8.5
1-2 years	9	19.1
3-5 years	5	10.6
6-10 years	6	12.8
11-15 years	3	6.4
16-20 years	1	2.1
21-life	9	19.1
	47	
Occupational Category		
Professional, managerial	2	4.3
Clerical, sales	1	2.2
Service	30	65.2
Farm, fishing, forestry, etc.	1	2.2
Processing	1	2.2
Machine trades	0	0.0
Bench work	0	0.0
Structural	4	8.7
Miscellaneous	2	4.3
Service and miscellaneous	4	8.7
Structural and miscellaneous	1	2.2
	46	
Skill Level		
Professional, managerial	2	4.3
Technical	0	0.0
Skilled	11	23.9
Unskilled	18	39.1
Semiskilled	3	6.5
Semi- or unskilled	12	26.1
	46	

Table 77

Last Full-Time Job Experience

Last Full-Time Job	N	Percent
Part- or Full-Time		
Full-time	43	81.1
Seasonal	10	18.9
	53	
Duration		
Under 6 months	6	13.0
6 months to 1 year	3	6.5
1-2 years	8	17.4
3-5 years	8	17.4
6-10 years	2	4.3
11-15 years	4	8.7
16-20 years	3	6.5
21-life	12	26.1
	46	
Occupational Category		
Professional, managerial, technical	4	8.3
Clerical, sales	3	6.2
Service	17	35.4
Farm, fishing, forestry, etc.	4	8.3
Processing	4	8.3
Machine trades	0	0.0
Bench work	0	0.0
Structural work	7	14.6
Miscellaneous	7	14.6
Service and miscellaneous	1	2.1
Structural and miscellaneous	1	2.1
	48	
Skill Level		
Professional, managerial	4	8.5
Skilled	14	29.8
Semiskilled	13	27.7
Semiskilled or unskilled	7	14.9
Unskilled	9	19.1
	47	

Table 78

Relationship Between Occupational
Category of Last Job and Feeling
Toward School

		Category	
Feeling Toward School	Service	Others	Total
Positive	18	3	21
Not positive	9	11	20
Total	27	14	41

Yates χ^2 = 5.849, df = 1, $p < 0.016$

Table 79

Relationship Between Last Full-Time
or Part-Time Job and Activities as a
Youth

		Last Job	
Number of Activities as a Youth	Full-Time	Part-Time (daily)	Total
0, 1, 4 or more	5	23	28
2-3	10	10	20
Total	15	33	48

χ^2 = 5.610, df = 1, $p < 0.02$

or twice a month at the maximum. The remaining men reported working regularly at "spot jobs" once a week or more. Nearly 60 percent had not held a regular full-time position for anywhere from one year to over twenty years and many had not even taken "spot" labor for six months or more. For subjects reporting having held their last full-time job sometime during the past year, both parents

Table 80

**Relationship Between Skill of Last Job
and First Phase of Alcohol Dependence**

| Alcohol Dependence in First Phase | Skill of Last Job | | Total |
	Skilled or Better	Semi- or Unskilled	
Heavy	3	21	24
Light-moderate	10	10	20
Total	13	31	44

Yates $\chi^2 = 5.678$, $df = 1$, $p < 0.017$

Table 81

**Relationship Between Skill of Last Job
and Second Phase of Alcohol Dependence**

| Alcohol Dependence in Second Phase | Skill of Last Job | | Total |
	Skilled or Better	Semi- or unskilled	
Heavy	7	30	37
Light-moderate	6	2	8
Total	13	32	45

Yates $\chi^2 = 7.525$, $df = 1$, $p < 0.006$

Table 82

**Factors Involved in Subjects' Present
Motivation to Work**

Work Orientation	N	Percent
Still Looking for Work		
Looking (at least once a week)	20	48.8
Not looking	9	22.0
Not looking due to chronic physical condition	12	29.3
	41	
Hours Per Week Desired		
Full-time	23	74.2
Part-time	8	25.8
	31	

Table 82 (*continued*)

Work Orientation	N	Percent
Knowledge of Where or How to Look for Work		
MP, LP (Manpower, Labor Pool)	13	38.2
Employment agencies (alone or in combination)	8	23.5
Direct to employer (alone or in combination)	10	29.4
Center, friends, "They come to me."	3	8.8
	34	
Extent of Work in Past 6 Months or Since Last Full-Time Job		
None	17	31.5
Infrequent	8	14.8
1-2/week	6	11.1
3-4/week	8	14.8
?/week	13	24.1
Nearly full-time	2	3.7
	54	
Present Employment		
None or less than 1/week	36	72.0
Not employed, but works 1-2/week	4	8.0
3-4/week regularly	6	12.0
33 hours or more	4	8.0
	50	
How Long Ago Last Full-Time Job		
Under 6 months	12	27.9
6 months to under 1 year	6	13.9
1-2 years	8	18.6
3-5 years	9	20.9
6-10 years	2	4.6
11-15 years	5	11.6
16-20 years	0	0.0
21-life	1	2.3
	43	
How Long Ago Last Job		
Under 6 months	12	54.5
6 months to 1 year	3	13.6
1-2 years	2	9.1
3-4 years	5	22.7
	22	

tended to have been present during their first 17 years. This relationship is presented in Table 83. For subjects who were

Table 83

**Relationship Between Time Since Last
Full-Time Job and Parental Loss**

	Time Since Last Full-Time Job		
Parental Loss	Through 1 year	Over 1 year to life	Total
No	12	8	20
Yes	6	16	22
Total	18	24	42

Yates χ^2 = 3.343, df = 1, p < 0.068

presently employed on a regular basis and generally worked at least two days a week, favoritism toward the subject or toward any other family member had not been displayed by either the mother or the father. These relationships are presented in Tables 84 and 85.

Table 84

**Relationship Between Present Employ-
ment and Mother's Favorite Child**

	Extent of Present Employment		
Mother's Favorite Child	< 1/week	Regular, > 1/week	Total
No favorite	3	5	8
Subject, not subject	14	2	16
Total	17	7	24

Yates χ^2 = 4.26, df = 1, p < 0.05

Table 85

**Relationship Between Present Employ-
ment and Father's Favorite Child**

| | Extent of Present Employment | | |
Father's Favorite Child	$<1/week$	Regular, $>1/week$	Total
No favorite	3	5	8
Not subject	6	0	6
Total	9	5	14

Fisher Exact (2-tail) = 0.028

Similarly, subjects who worked consistently, whether daily or full
time, since their last full-time job had perceived no favoritism
expressed by their mother. This relationship is presented in Table 86.

Table 86

**Relationship Between Work Since Last
Full-Time Job and Mother's Favorite
Child**

| | Work Since Last Full-Time Job | | |
Mother's Favorite Child	None-or not consistently	Daily, full-time (consistently)	Total
No favorite, subject	6	13	19
Not subject	7	1	8
Total	13	14	27

Yates χ^2 = 4.98, df = 1, $p < 0.05$

The only relationship observed between early social experience and
recent motivation to work involved activities as a youth and time
since last full-time job. Subjects who had been involved in a

moderate number of activities outside the home tended to be those whose last full-time employment occurred within the past year. This relationship is presented in Table 87.

Table 87

Relationship Between Time Since Last
Full-Time Job and Number of Activities
as a Youth

Number of Activities	Time Since Last Full-Time Job		Total
	Through 1 year	Over 1 year to life	
0, 1, 4 or more	6	17	23
2-3	10	6	16
Total	16	23	39

$$\chi^2 = 5.17, df = 1, p < 0.05$$

Implications of Rehabilitation

Adequate vocational placement as soon as the alcohol dependent is ready is almost imperative. His self-concept relative to his adequacy and value requires the support of achievement and productivity of work, particularly in our culture which is so achievement oriented and equates masculinity with the capacity to earn a living and support oneself. Further, it is important that the rehabilitation counselor do more than see that the alcohol dependent is placed; he must also work with him toward eventually achieving a job of some degree of status and at the highest level of his ability.

Note, the phrase "eventually achieving a job . . . at the highest level of his ability" is used. The word "eventually" is crucial. It is suggested that the achievement of maximum vocational status should take place in a series of transitional steps. The data show that those alcohol dependents whose first job experience was of a full-time, final nature were the least successful in vocational advancement and more dependent on alcohol. Immediate placement in a final low-status job causes the individual to feel in a rut; yet, if the job makes difficult demands, the alcohol dependent will not be able to tolerate the stress.

The interests of the alcohol dependent might best be served if he occupies a series of two or three positions of increasing difficulty or stress. This procedure will not only provide him with the opportunity to develop increasing work tolerance for responsibility but also afford him an opportunity to achieve experience in adjusting to changing and differing interpersonal demands so that his capacity for social negotiation and adaptation is increased. Naturally, the alcohol dependent will mobilize much anxiety during these job changes and will require much in the way of emotional support and a certain amount of intervention in his behalf by the rehabilitation counselor.

The rehabilitation counselor's efforts must be directed not only toward the alcohol dependent but toward his employer. In most cases the employer starts out with little understanding of the alcohol dependent's problems and finds it difficult to tolerate and accept his abberant behavior. The counselor must build a relationship with the employer based upon confidence so that his interpretations of the alcohol dependent's actions will be accepted and acted upon. A survey by Margolin (1955) illustrated the value of a series of graduated transitional steps to final job placement of severe schizophrenics. He stressed the value of constant interpretation of the client's behavior.

The importance of vocation in contributing to self-actualization as defined by Maslow (1954) is suggested by the data. Subjects who worked on the railroad, were steeple jacks, or had businesses or professions of any kind gave evidence of the importance of these vocations in giving a meaning to their lives. Hence, the placement of the alcohol dependent client in job situations which are self-actualizing could prove to be a strong motivational factor in helping the alcohol dependent to reduce his dependency upon alcohol. A meaningful job forms a paramount part of an individual's identity. Since the identity of the alcohol dependent is fragmented or at best poorly formed, an adequate vocational identification is helpful in identity restoration.

If the establishment of priorities for rehabilitation based upon feasibility becomes a factor, the rehabilitation professional is faced with a dilemma. The alcohol dependents with the better family backgrounds and higher-level vocational histories drank less and had the more developed social skills that make for better rehabilitation potential. However, those with the lower-level vocational backgrounds and poorer backgrounds, from a family and social-dynamics point of view, had more favorable attitudes toward treatment resources. The answer may be the capacity of particular rehabilitation agencies to extend offers of rehabilitation treatment to the better prospects in a way that is more rewarding and appeals to motivation for greater occupational and social potential.

On the other hand, the heavy drinkers among the alcohol dependents with poor educational backgrounds, when motivated for treatment, could probably benefit from educational therapy. Such therapy contributes to the self-actualizing process. Weiss and Margolin (1969) and Rudd and Margolin (1970) have indicated in some detail the value of educational therapy as a motivating force and as a means of achieving improved personality functioning.

Few would deny the therapeutic potential of work. However, although this is recognized, it is not infrequently considered unfeasible to attempt rehabilitation of the alcohol dependent client following several work failures. Initial failure may well be part of the alcohol dependent's behavior pattern. Only through repeated trials can a measure of success be achieved.

9 Psychdiagnostic and
Behavioral Indices of
Dependency

To review briefly, three psychodiagnostic paper and pencil tests and
six behavioral tasks were administered to the subjects during the first
of the two sessions for the purpose of obtaining measures of
characteristic and situational dependency, respectively. The psychodiagnostic tests used were: (1) the Navran (Dy) Scale for ascertaining
the level of dependence as a personality trait of characteristic mode
of behavior; (2) the Marlowe-Crowne scale for assessing social
desirability or the extent to which social behavior is conditioned by
the norms of society; and (3) the Predicament Story Test (Schwaab,
1959) for determining conflict over the need to be dependent when
dependence is present.

Six behavioral tasks were administered: (1) the presentation of
two Rorschach cards for assessing the relative ease or difficulty with
which a person of a measured degree of characteristic dependence is
able to respond to a new stimulus situation of a relatively
unstructured nature by defining it; (2) the presentation of two TAT
cards for ascertaining the relative ease or difficulty with which a
person of a measured degree of characteristic dependence is able to
respond to a new stimulus situation of a relatively *structured* nature
by defining it; (3) the presentation of two "number judgement"
tasks, involving, in addition to the variable structure, a form of risk
or consequence resulting from the decision, for ascertaining the
relative amount of information needed by the more and less
characteristically dependent person before he would feel "secure"
enough to make a decision for which a consequence of his choice
would result; (4) the presentation of a "near-impossible" puzzle task
for determining the extent to which persons of a measured degree of
characteristic dependency will ask for help in solving the problem;
(5) presentation of the Welsh Figure Preference test for assessing the
relative appeal of visual stimuli varying in structure from the highly
structured geometric design to the almost completely abstract form
to persons of a measured degree of characteristic dependency; and
(6) the presentation of the Drawing Completion Test for assessing
the relative flexibility-rigidity of approach utilized by persons with
measured levels of characteristic dependency. For a more thorough
review of the methodology, the reader is referred to Chapter 3.

Frequency Distributions

Psychodiagnostic Indices

Navran (Dy) Scale. A Dy score was obtained for each subject by summing the number of true-false statements answered, according to a scoring key, in such a way as to reflect dependency. The mean Dy score based upon 55 tests was 29.5 with a standard deviation of 11.1. The scores ranged from 9 to 48 (with a possible score of 57). The median fell at 29.0.

Marlowe-Crowne Social Desirability Scale (SD). An SD score was obtained for each subject by summing the number of true-false statements answered in such a way, according to a scoring key, as to indicate the need for social approval. The mean SD score, based upon 55 tests, was 18.5 with a standard deviation of 6.35. The scores ranged from 4 to 32 (with a possible high score of 33). The median fell at 19.0.

Predicament Story Test (PST). Each answer for the 18-question multiple-choice test is classified as a +2, +1, 0, −1, or −2 depending upon which of the 5 alternatives was chosen. In turn, the total number of answers falling within each of the 5 categories is computed. These observed frequencies are then compared to the derived expected frequencies reported by Schwaab and subjects are assigned to the appropriate conflict or nonconflict group. The results based upon the test scores of 48 subjects are shown in Table 88 together with the derived expected frequencies obtained by Schwaab.

Behavioral Measures

TAT Cards. The range of response times to the first (6BM) and second (20) cards presented were 3 to 115 seconds and 3 to 125 seconds, respectively. Based upon 55 and 54 subjects, the means, medians, and standard deviations, in that order, were: 18.0, 14.0, and 17.8 seconds to the first card; 19.4, 13.5, and 20.8 seconds to the second card.

Rorschach Cards. Response times to the first (sixth) and second (ninth) Rorschach cards ranged from 1 to 83 seconds and from 1 to 185 seconds, respectively. Based upon 54 subjects, mean, medians,

Table 88

Observed Frequencies (f^{ob}) of
Occurrence of PST Scores in Four
Subgroups of Conflicted and
Nonconflicted Subjects and Schwaab's
Derived Expected Frequencies (f^{ex})
of PST Scores

				Score		
Group		+2	+1	0	−1	−2
Acceptors (N=13)	f^{ob}	3.20	2.70	1.80	3.40	6.90
	f^{ex}	1.20	2.40	3.60	4.80	6.00
Deniers (N=18)	f^{ob}	6.70	3.80	2.20	2.70	2.60
	f^{ex}	6.00	4.80	3.60	2.40	1.20
Vacillator (N=1)	f^{ob}	1.00	3.00	8.00	3.00	3.00
	f^{ex}	1.00	4.00	6.00	4.00	1.00
Nonconflicted (N=16)	f^{ob}	2.80	5.50	2.70	4.00	2.60
	f^{ex}	1.00	6.00	4.00	6.00	1.00

and standard deviations, in that order, were: 15.2, 7.5, and 17.2 seconds to the first card; 26.4, 15.5, and 31.0 seconds to the second card.

Letter "M" Puzzle. The median number of responses made by subjects while they attempted to form a letter of the alphabet with the given wooden pieces was 8, the first response occurring on the average at one minute. (The puzzle was not successfully solved by anyone within the given time period). Two of the 55 subjects made no response during the 10-minute period.

In terms of response content, 42 or 79 percent of the 53 subjects who responded asked for information, with the first such response occurring on the average at slightly over 2 minutes. Thirty-nine, or 74 percent of the 53 subjects who responded, expressed feelings of defeat, with the first defeat response occurring on the average at nearly 4 minutes. Blame responses were emitted by 25 or 47 percent of the 53 subjects who responded, with the first such response occurring on the average at slightly over 3.5 minutes.

The summary statistics are presented in Table 89. With the exception of number of responses, all distributions are skewed to the

Table 89

Summary Statistics for Response Times and Number of Responses Made While Working on the Letter "M" Puzzle

| | Response Time (secs.) | | |
Response	Mean	Median	Standard Deviation
(Number of Responses (N=53)	8.4	8.0	4.6)
First Response Time (N=53)	61.6	42.0	76.4
First Information Response (N=42)	128.8	67.5	149.4
First Blame Response (N=25)	159.2	110.0	150.3
First Defeat Response (N=39)	238.5	180.0	140.8

left and account for the discrepancies between mean and median response times.

Of the 53 subjects who made at least one response while working on the puzzle, 79.2 percent asked for information, 23.6 percent expressed defeat, and 47.2 percent blamed themselves or some outside source for their inability to solve the problem, the large majority placing the blame solely upon themselves.

Number Judgment. The range in number of cards requested, including the first 5 "free" cards, for the first and second number judgment tasks were 4 to 25 and 3 to 25 cards, respectively (25 was the maximum number shown). Based on 55 subjects, the means, medians, and standard deviations were: 12.6, 11.0, and 6.1 for the first task; 11.2, 10.0, and 5.3 for the second task.

Welsh Figure Preference. The response measure used was the number of expansive or more abstract figures preferred for the first 4 out of 8 figures shown. Twenty-nine percent of the subjects chose all 4 highly structured geometric designs in their first 4 choices and were consequently assigned the score of 0. Twenty-two percent chose one expansive figure in their first 4 choices, 27 percent chose 2, 18 percent chose 3, and only 4 percent chose all 4 abstract designs as their first 4 preferences. Based upon 55 subjects the mean number of abstract figures preferred was 1.4, with a standard deviation of 1.2. The median fell at 1.0.

Drawing-Completion Test. Tests were scored on 5-point scale from 0 to 4, with the low end of the scale reflecting an inflexible approach to the stimulus lines and the high end indicative of a flexible expansive approach to the task. Seventy-one percent of the subjects were assigned the score of 0 to 1. Eleven percent introduced some complexity and asymmetry into their drawings and expanded beyond the given lines to some extent and were assigned the score of 2. The remaining 18 percent, scoring 3 and 4, illustrated in many of their drawings considerable creativity in approach. Based upon 55 subjects, the mean score was 1.4 with a standard deviation of 1.0. The median fell at 1.0.

Support for Hypotheses

Psychodiagnostic Indices

That alcohol dependents would score substantially higher on the Navran (Dy) Scale than did the 200 "normals" upon whom Navran based his norms. The hypothesis was supported. The mean obtained by Navran for a sample of 200 Minnesota "normals" was 19.0 with a standard deviation of 8.3. The mean Dy score for the 55 alcohol dependents was 29.5 with a standard deviation of 11.1. (For Navran's group of 29 nonhospitalized neurotics the mean was 29.6 with a standard deviation of 11.5).

That alcohol dependents would score substantially higher on the Marlowe-Crowne Social Desirability Scale than did the 666 male undergraduate psychology students upon whom the Marlowe-Crowne norms are based. The hypothesis was not supported. The mean reported by Marlowe and Crowne was 15.1 with a standard deviation of 5.6. The mean SD score for the 55 alcohol dependents was 18.5 with a standard deviation of 6.35. Although the mean score obtained for the alcohol dependents was higher, the difference was not significant.

That alcohol dependents would be classified substantially more often as conflicted over their need for dependence, as opposed to nonconflicted, on the Predicament Story Test. The hypothesis was supported. Thirty-seven or 69.8 percent of the alcohol dependents were classified as in conflict over their need for dependence while only 16 or 30.2 percent were classified as nonconflicted. Of those who evidenced conflict, 34.0 percent were classified as dependency "deniers" while 24.5 percent and 1.9 percent were classified as dependency "acceptors" and "vacillators," respectively. Five subjects who favored not one but both extremes were arbitrarily classified as "acceptors-deniers" (a comparable group was not reported by Schwaab).

Thus, the nonconflicted group favored neither extreme but fell most frequently between +1 and −1; the vacillator fell at the midpoint (0) denoting indecision; the deniers fell at the extreme (+2) representing independent action; the acceptors fell at the opposite extreme (−2) signifying dependent action; Choice of either extreme represents the least realistic solution to the predicament-the "I am an island" approach used by the denier and the "If I am obedient, I will always be safe" philosophy employed by the acceptor. The vacillator does not come to a solution at all. The five acceptors-deniers and the single vacillator were not considered in subsequent analyses.

Behavioral Measures

No predictions were made for TAT, Rorschach, and number-judgment performance because of the lack of comparison data.

That alcohol dependents would display help-seeking behavior on the Letter "M" Puzzle. The hypothesis was not supported. In general, subjects sought structure but not direct requests for help concerning the disposition of the unstructured near-impossible puzzle task. The requests for information (e.g., "how much time do I have?") which, when not filled, were replaced by blame responses directed primarily toward themselves, and finally by defeat responses (verbal and/or nonverbal expressions of failure without blame).

That alcohol dependents would prefer structured rather than abstract figures on the Welsh Figure Preference. The hypothesis was confirmed. Slightly over 75 percent of the subjects preferred 2 or fewer of the more abstract figures presented. The mean number of abstract figures preferred was 1.4 (of a possible 4). On the average, then, subjects tended to prefer the regular, orderly, static figures to the irregular, disorderly, dynamic ones.

That alcohol dependents would display more rigidity than flexibility in approach to the Drawing Completion Test. The hypothesis was supported. The same tendencies were observed for the Drawing Completion Test as were observed for the Welsh Figure Preference. As will be recalled, the former task required simple preference whereas the Drawing Completion Test called for active expression. Of a possible score of 5 points, the average score for the alcohol dependents was 1.4. Rather than elaborating on the simple figures, the subjects chose for the most part to simply connect lines and close in figures.

Discussion of Response Distributions

The alcohol dependents scored substantially higher on the Navran Dependence Scale than did a "representative sample of the general population" ($N = 200$). In fact, the mean score for the fifty five alcohol dependents was identical to that obtained for twenty nine nonhospitalized outpatient "neurotics," and similar to that of a group of neuropsychiatric patients also reported by Navran. If the Navran Dy Scale measures characteristic dependency, then it must be concluded that the alcohol dependents evidenced considerable dependency in the psychological sense.

Not only did they manifest characteristic dependency but the majority were classified as conflicted over their need to be dependent by the Predicament Story Test. Over half of those in conflict could be described as dependency "deniers" who attempt to resolve their conflict through reaction formation, an ego defense, by outwardly behaving overly independent. Most of the remaining subjects in conflict over their need to be dependent were classified as dependency "acceptors." Rather than deny their conflict, they attempt to behave in an independent manner through identification with a nondependent person who essentially performs independent acts for them. As suggested by the literature and pointed out earlier, dependency and, more importantly, conflict over the need to be dependent can play a significant role in the etiology of alcohol dependency.

Although it was expected that alcohol dependents would score relatively high on the Marlowe-Crown SD Scale, the results did not support this expectation. Nor did the data suggest that, because these skid-rowers had rejected many of the norms and values of the larger society, their perceived need for social approval was substantially lower than that of other groups still participating in the larger society. All that can be concluded is that the alcohol dependents did not display overconcern or underconcern for the norms of society relative to their behavior in the social sense.

Although the expected help-seeking behavior was not displayed during the attempted solution of the Letter "M" Puzzle, more than three-quarters of the alcohol dependents did ask for some structure to the near-impossible task and expressed defeat when the solution was not forthcoming. The desire for structure was expressed on the average at one minute and feelings of failure at about four minutes. Further, a full half expressed feelings of inadequacy in the face of this difficult problem situation in the form of self-blame (e.g., "I am so dumb") after working on the puzzle for, on the average, only two and one half minutes. After direct requests for help were not made, it was evident that when confronted with a difficult situation these alcohol dependents would require considerable support and building of ego strength if they were to eventually overcome obstacles.

Assuming that behavior on the Letter "M" Puzzle represents, in general, the approach used by alcohol dependents to solve difficult problems in real life, let us look at what might happen to the alcohol dependent's attempt to resolve his dependency on alcohol. He is told by his rehabilitation counselor or by AA members that he must abstain from drinking (presentation of the problem). Initially, he makes every effort to stop, but in time doubt takes over and he becomes convinced of his ultimate failure to stop drinking. No help is offered and he is not able to ask for help (after all, he does not need help — if he really wanted to stop drinking, he could!) Instead, the doubts increase and soon he is finding all sorts of reasons to support his feelings of unworthiness and self-hate (self-blame). He gives up (is defeated) and returns to the bottle to restore his feelings of well-being and bolster his ego. The battle is over.

Performance on the Welsh Figure Preference and Drawing Completion Test further supports the thesis that the alcohol dependent has considerable difficulty in dealing with the unstructured and approaching the unstructured in a flexible way. Concurrent with the goal of building ego strength must necessarily be the goal of reducing the strength of the vast and powerful network of defense mechanisms, initially erected to enable the alcohol dependent to better cope within his fearful milieu.

Due to the absence of data with which response times on the TAT and Rorschach could be compared, it was impossible to assess the ability of the alcohol dependents to respond to new stimulus situations. Responses to all four cards occurred, on the average, within half a minute, a seemingly short time. Among the possible explanations are lack of motivation or refusal to deal with the stimulus situations in other than a superficial manner. Similarly, decision making on the Number Judgment tasks in which some risk as a consequence of the decision was involved (loss of highly prized cigarettes) was difficult to assess without a comparison criterion.

Behavioral vs. Biographical Variables

Parametric tests of significance (*t* test and *F* test) were performed on situational (performance) measures of dependency with life-style indices of dependency serving as criterion measures. In addition, nonparametric tests of significance (chi square tests) were used to determine relationships between behavioral and biographical variables. Because of the small cell frequencies in the case of chi square analyses, all tables were fourfold.

For performance on the Rorschach, TAT, and Number Judgment tasks, and for the number of responses and time of first response for the Letter "M" Puzzle, the top and bottom quarters of the response distributions were combined for *HL* vs. *M* comparisons. For time of first information, blame, and defeat responses to the Letter "M" Puzzle, table cells were collapsed in the direction of cell frequencies. For the Welsh Figure Preference and Drawing Completion Test, comparisons were made between high scorers (scores of 2, 3, and 4) and low scorers (scores of 0 and 1).

Because of the extremely small number of significant relationships observed relative to the number of relationships tested, as well as inconsistencies among the findings themselves both in terms of content and direction, it was concluded that the probability of chance occurrence of significance was high. For this reason a presentation of significant relationships and trends will not be presented.

Implications for Rehabilitation

The data in this chapter further support the assumption that the individual dependent upon alcohol is also psychosocially dependent in terms of psychodiagnostic measurement. Thus, the Navran Scale from the MMPI might have value in assessing the initial level of dependency of the client so that the counselor may plan the pace of his demands for independent functioning during the rehabilitation process.

Since the findings suggest that the alcohol dependent is in conflict over his dependent strivings, the importance of helping the alcohol user is indicated. After the alcohol dependent has been helped to confront his conflict over dependency, he can then be motivated to begin to redirect his dependency needs toward more acceptable objects.

Perhaps the most important finding is the alcohol dependent's need for structure. In all aspects of the alcohol dependent's rehabilitation this need for structure cannot be ignored. This applies to nonresidential as well as residential rehabilitation services. Since lack of structure in the alcohol dependent's milieu probably engenders anxiety, he should be initially afforded the protection of much structure and direction in his life space.

There is considerable difference between acceptance and permissiveness. The alcohol dependent must be accepted as a personality with integrity, while directiveness can be so used that ambivalence does not paralyze his activities. Thus, although decisions cannot be made for the alcohol dependent, much can be achieved if, at least initially, some intervention takes place to help enable him to make his own decisions. As he becomes capable of functioning amid less structure, the rehabilitation worker can become less directive. In residential rehabilitation settings the importance of routine systematic living should be stressed as a means of providing a measure of structured security for the alcohol dependent client.

10 Summary and Implications for Rehabilitation

It is the purpose of this chapter to summarize and further interpret the data gathered in this study and to discuss its significance for the field of rehabilitation from the standpoints of practice, administration, planning, and research. Specific suggestions will be made for the revision of psychosocial rehabilitation treatment techniques for the alcohol dependent, for modification of existing facilities, and for the creation of new rehabilitative facilities. Concern will be with the concepts directly relevant to the rehabilitation of the alcohol dependent client.

Data from the study can be summarized as follows:

1. A substantial proportion of the alcohol dependents sustained emotional losses in their lives. Such losses were represented by low parental availability or parental absence through death, divorce, or separation, etc. Not infrequently, similar losses recurred later in their lives through loss of spouse or fiancee or loss of a vocation or business in which the alcohol dependent had a strong ego investment and which symbolically had become a love object.

2. A substantial proportion of the alcohol dependents had dominant and, in some cases, overprotective mothers. In combination with alcohol dependent or absent fathers, an emotional configuration in the family detrimental to the subjects' development of an adequate masculine identification may have been produced.

3. A substantial proportion of the alcohol dependents had limited experience in the development of social interaction skills during their childhood and early adolescence in community activities or within the school setting. Since the lack of social interaction in the early lives of the alcohol dependents was associated with the presence of a controlling mother (decision maker) one can speculate upon the role of the mother in blocking social interaction of the subject. His possible use of alcohol later in life may have been a means of reducing tensions engendered by the social situations in which he found himself. Moreover, alcohol might have served as a compensation for the lack of experienced social satisfactions. It is interesting to note the lack of social participation associated with heavier drinking.

4. The alcohol dependents who had not had treatment for their alcohol addiction tended to be those with little in the way of early social interaction experiences. One can speculate on the inability of the alcohol dependent to involve himself in the social negotiations required to seek, acquire, and sustain treatment.

5. Forty-two percent of the sample were suffering from a chronic ailment or disability other than alcohol dependency. While this chronic illness did not usually prevent employment, it did limit the type and quantity of work which these alcohol dependents could do (25 percent of the subjects reported not looking for work because of a chronic condition).

6. Most of the alcohol dependent subjects were able to obtain jobs and work regularly at jobs with some degree of stability during many periods in their lives.

7. Those subjects who had early social experiences in school and in the community showed more competency in their vocational histories.

8. Dependence on alcohol was far greater among those subjects who throughout their lives, from their first work experience to their last, had been employed in positions requiring little in the way of skill and competency.

9. Alcohol dependents in the research population evidenced a high prevalence of nonmarriage. Those who did marry had a difficult time in maintaining the marital relationship, which usually ended in divorce or separation.

Implications for Rehabilitation Counseling

These findings have a number of basic implications for the rehabilitation of the alcohol dependent. One treatment modality which has been shown to be of value is counseling. The findings suggest that the relationship established between counselor and alcohol dependent must be a close dependent one, initially. Rehabilitation counseling, as we know it, is comprised of three major dimensions:

1. Assisting the client in the determination of a diagnostically based plan for raising his level of functioning.
2. Mobilizing and coordinating community (medical, social psychological and vocational) resources in the client's behalf.

3. Providing the client with a supportive (psychotherapeutic) relationship to maintain motivation and reduce dependency.

All three functions of the rehabilitation counselor are important. Yet, in the rehabilitation of the alcohol dependent, the maintenance of a supportive relationship is primary. If the client has sustained a sequence of emotional loss which has contributed to his dependency, he may require a type of emotional replacement therapy which can be supplied by the rehabilitation counselor. By allowing an initially strong dependent relationship to develop, the counselor can compensate to some degree for the lost love objects in the life of the alcoholic client.

In most counseling or casework relationships the fostering of dependency is often frowned upon. However, in the rehabilitation of the alcohol dependent, such a relationship should not be discouraged. At the outset, the client requires the counselor's unconditional support. he should then be gradually weaned from this dependent relationship. The findings indicate that repeatedly, from early childhood, such support has been withdrawn either due to acts of fate or humanly contrived conditions.

Kaufman and Heims (1958) described what they call a depressive nucleus in the personalities of juvenile delinquents which they feel results from early emotional loss or rejection. Evidence from this study suggests that a similar configuration is a component of the alcohol dependent personality. The alcohol dependent drinks as a way of dealing with his depression and substitutes liquor for love. The counselor's complete concern for the client and the allowance of a total type of dependent relationship, in essence, takes the counselee back to the time of his first loss and provides him with a stable object to support his dependent strivings.

After initial acceptance of the childish dependency, the counselor is in a position to begin the weaning process. Once the initial total dependency stage is reached and a strong supportive relationship is attained, the counselor can establish the treatment agreement which will govern the future conduct of the treatment course. The counselor makes it clear that, if the alcohol dependent client really wants to stop drinking and to rejoin society, the counselor has some knowledge, skill, and legitimated authority and commitment to help him do so. Moreover, the counselor demonstrates his willingness to give total committment to the task. In addition, it is made clear that, while he may not always accept the client's actions, he will always accept the client himself and under no circumstances withdraw his support. In other words, he must be able to reassure the client against another emotional loss.

Conveying the assurance against loss to the client is a complex and difficult task. The loss patterns are deeply etched upon the alcohol dependent's unconscious. The formation of another deep emotional relationship, only to have it withdrawn, is a constant threat to the alcohol dependent person. Observations have been made of the frequent shallowness of relationships of the confirmed alcohol addict. We speculate that this difficulty in forming relationships is due, at least in part, to unconscious anxiety over the possibility of recurrence of initial emotional loss.

The rehabilitation counselor must be prepared for the drinking episodes. These may occur for many reasons. One reason is the client's use of his own drinking behavior to test the counselor's total committment to him. Without realizing it, he drinks to ascertain whether or not the counselor will reject him because of it before he further commits himself to a deeper relationship which might end in another emotional loss. A second reason is fear of relinquishing his dependent mode of functioning as the counselor begins to make slight demands of him for independence. By drinking, he again reverts to a state of total dependency (oral-infantile) upon the counselor. A third reason for drinking episodes may be related to a form of self-punishment (masochistic) in which the client persists because of feeling of guilt and unworthiness of the counselor's total committment to him. The counselor's giving of himself may arouse the client's guilt, and so he punishes himself and simultaneously attempts to drive the rehabilitation counselor away.

Coping with feelings of inadequacy and guilt are primary problems in the rehabilitation counselor's treatment of the client dependent upon alcohol, for they are concomitant with emotional loss. In the irrational and magical thinking which is characteristic of the unconscious processes, rejection and loss are frequently interpreted as punishment for wrong, forbidden deeds or as a symbolic confirmation of inadequacy. In other words, "I am rejected or left out because I am not wanted . . . therefore, I am unworthy of love or something is wrong with me."

This phase in which the counseling relationship is being formed, tested, and solidified is a difficult hurdle for both client and counselor. It will frequently require an extended period of time — six months, a year, perhaps longer. However, once this phase is successfully negotiated, the goals of the counseling process can be clearly defined with the client. Then rehabilitation goals can be worked toward in earnest. These goals are:

1. Reduction of dependency upon alcohol.
2. The reentry of the alcohol dependent into the normative framework of society.
3. Regular employment.

It must be borne in mind that the rehabilitation of the alcohol dependent is a process which requires counseling over an extended period of time. The alcoholic behavior pattern requires time for its evolvement and requires time to be extinguished.

One possible method to reduce dependency upon alcohol involves the use of a system calling for *increasing sobriety period targets.* For the counselor to ask the client to stop drinking permanently and completely would merely serve to increase his anxiety relative to expected failure. This would overwhelm him. Instead, the counselor and client mutually agree upon a target period during which the client will not drink. To begin with, these periods are short — a day, three days, a week, ten days, etc.

If the individual makes it through the sobriety target period without drinking, another slightly longer sobriety period is agreed upon, and gradually the length of these periods are increased. If the client drinks during the period, another time period is attempted. In this manner, the client's dependency upon alcohol as a mechanism to reduce anxiety and escape reality is reduced. In order that the strength of the counseling relationship may be continued, at no time should the client's failures be censured.

This method is suggested in view of those alcohol dependent subjects who did not always drink constantly but, rather, intermittently. That is, they went through periods when they did not drink, only to later return to their previous drinking habits or increased alcohol intake. The specific motivation for these intermittent drinking patterns was not clear from the data, although crisis situations frequently act as "drinking precipitators." In view of the alcohol dependent's ability to stop drinking for periods of time, a motivational relationship with the counselor assuming the role of a loss replacement surrogate might serve to appreciably extend these periods of sobriety. Perhaps, in some cases, total abstinence could be achieved.

As the alcohol dependent in rehabilitation counseling begins to achieve extended periods of sobriety, other dimensions of the rehabilitation process can be brought into play; namely, vocational counseling, training and placement. The client must also be assisted in reestablishing psychosocial contact with significant others in his community and family life. It must be remembered that, as the individual becomes increasingly more dependent on alcohol, he sustains a final emotional loss in the form of rejection by his family, friends, and the community. Thus, rejecting the norms and values of society and being rejected by them, he moves out of the mainstream of life.

The rehabilitation counselor who works with the alcohol dependent must counsel with his family members, former friends, and employer to interpret problems and help these significant others reaccept the client into their social systems. If the support and acceptance of the alcohol dependent cannot be obtained from these individuals, then adequately supportive and accepting "significant other surrogates" must be made available to the client. The importance of this phase of the counseling process is emphasized by the finding that many of the alcohol dependents had obtained only limited experience in the learning of social skills and had participated minimally in meaningful psychosocial transactions in community life. Lack of social interaction skills can be one contributing factor to alcohol dependency.

To the counselor, then, falls the task of helping the client to reinstate his family and/or community ties. Rejection by individuals from these social systems merely constitutes another emotional loss in an already painful loss sequence. The achievement of acceptance by significant others is a difficult process, because after the drinker passes a certain point in his social deviance (the point at which there is public loss of control of drinking), society isolates him. The counselor must also prepare those close to the alcohol dependent client for occasional drinking relapses. Indigenous nonprofessionals can assist the counselor in helping the alcohol dependent back to the mainstream of community life.

In providing emotional support for the client and carefully manipulating his environment, the counselor can motivate the client to transfer his oral dependency from the bottle to a dependent treatment relationship. Once this dependency transfer is effected, the counselor can attempt, over an extended period of time, to wean the counselee from his overdependent relationship with him. The key factor in this type of rehabilitation counseling is the counselor's capacity to remain on the case for a long period of time, perhaps for a period of several years. However, after the first year of intensive counseling, it is best for the counselor to see the client less frequently. The alcohol dependent must be made aware that the counselor has not withdrawn and severed his relationship with him but is available whenever he has the urge to return to drinking.

The client should be imbued with the response of calling or seeing his counselor whenever the urge to drink is compelling or when he has difficulty in coping with a stress situation. In this way he is provided with an ongoing partially dependent relationship to replace his early loss dependent status. This counseling pattern was used successfully with mentally ill patients by Margolin (1955) in the "Member Employee Program."

When first considered, the procedures outlined above may seem lengthy, cumbersome, expensive, and time consuming. However, upon closer examination, it becomes evident that following the initial intensive treatment phase the dependency "booster shots" provided require minimal time and effort on the part of the rehabilitation counselor.

A lack of emotional response by people close to them was evident in some of the biographies of the alcohol dependents. The extended type of counseling advocated provides the client with this needed "response." By "response" is meant the capacity of one individual to communicate to another individual his concern for and his understanding of what the other individual is feeling and living through. Not only has the alcohol dependent lost this "response" from significant others in his milieu, but, because of society's negative attitudes toward alcoholism, the societal system as a whole becomes almost totally unresponsive. Dependency is often looked upon as a destructive type of behavior.

Dependency upon the counselor in long-term extended counseling is used constructively as a stabilizing force against the use of alcohol. In the type of "extended rehabilitation counseling" described, the counselor serves to reinforce the decision of the client not to drink. We are led to speculate on the lack of goal direction in the decision making process of the alcohol dependent. Throughout his life he drifts into situations propelled by chance and circumstance rather than setting objectives and persisting in goal-directed behavior.

Thus, perhaps with the alcohol dependent client, counseling should take on a heavy decision making orientation, both in terms of working through to decisions and pursuing their implementation. His self-determinative capacity is in many cases weak. Therefore, the question of how directive the rehabilitation counselor should be becomes important. We speculate that alcohol dependents seek a strong parental figure or surrogate upon whom to be dependent. The counselor, therefore, can even forcefully be directive in making demands upon his client for meeting mutually established goals for abstinence, conformity, and productivity. If the counselor is able to accept the alcohol dependent's leaning upon him, he can convey his performance expectation to the client who in turn will seek to deliver on those expectations because of his need for the constructive dependent relationship with the counselor.

The potential value of rehabilitation counseling for the alcohol dependent is indicated by his strong need for human relationships. Even though he is quite alienated from society by the time he reaches the stage of strong dependency upon alcohol, he still has a need for psychosocial transactions and human acceptance (subjects in this study were frequently reluctant to have their interviews end). Frequently, the skid-row alcohol dependent is pictured as a torpid recluse so consumed by his alcohol pathology that he aspires to little or no communication with the world about him. This is untrue. The alcohol dependents in our research population not only appeared to achieve gratification from their social contact at the Salvation Army center but apparently achieved some need gratification from the relationships they formed with the researchers testing and interviewing them. While it was difficult for a few, many of the subjects appeared to achieve some type of therapeutic relief in talking with our interviewers.

In summing up, the major principles involved in counseling with the alcohol dependent can be stated as follows.

1. In helping the client set up his milieu or life space the counselor should aim initially to reduce psychological and social stress as much as possible. The findings indicate that stress frequently serves as a precipitating force in triggering off drinking behavior. Naturally, it is not possible to insulate the drinker completely from stress. However, in helping him select a job, for example, positions involving the stress of constant decision making can be initially ruled out. The client's tolerance for stress and conflict is built up in a gradual and graduated manner by the counselor's intervention in the initial control of the client's social environment.

2. The counselor should be constantly prepared to intervene quickly and positively to help the problem drinker deal with the crisis. Our

data show that the chronic drinker has had difficulty in coping with life crises which more independent individuals cope with without major personality disintegration. In time of crisis, it is necessary for the alcohol dependent to have the counselor to lean upon (even during what seems to be minor crises).

3. The counselor must become a long-term object of the chronic drinker's dependency, which over time is reduced by a gradual weaning process.

4. The counselor must actually teach the client social skills and provide opportunity and experiences to practice such skills (such group dynamics techniques as role playing are helpful).

When reading these guidelines it may seem as if an artificial world is being specially constructed for the client to insulate him from reality. This is not the case. Many subjects addicted to alcohol have repeatedly had emotional support withdrawn from them and we must never lose sight of this dramatic finding. Emotional losses contribute to a personality structure which is highly dependent and fragile. Direct demands for independent functioning will only precipitate further drinking. Therefore, it is important to allow initial dependency which is gradually reduced.

The findings point to the importance of highly skillful vocational counseling and placement in rehabilitating alcohol dependent clients. Interview material suggests for many the presence of a family emotional configuration which tends to interfere with needed masculine identification. In our achievement-oriented culture, work is symbolically equated with adequacy. Thus, a successful work experience can serve to bolster feelings of masculine adequacy. It seems desirable to reiterate that subjects with the more stable and successful work histories drank less than those with less consistently rewarding work experiences.

Transitional Residential Systems

Not all alcohol dependents can be treated while living in the open community. Some have reached a level of dependency so regressed that their ego functioning has hit the point of steady disintegration. They are dangerously self-destructive and quite incapable of adequately meeting their own reality needs. One example of this level of alcohol dependency is the addict who drinks toxic alcohol-containing compounds such as "canned heat." Another example was the subject who spent a winter night with two companions in a drunken stupor sleeping in an abandoned building. The subject's legs were seriously frozen and his two companions actually froze to death.

When alcohol dependents reach this point of dependency where they are incapable of self-care, some form of residential treatment is required for their rehabilitation. Residential treatment does not merely refer to an institution specializing in the "drying out" process, i.e., withdrawing the individual from alcohol through the use of drugs. It refers to a residential setting concerned with the total rehabilitation of the alcohol dependent and able to provide individual and group counseling as well as a milieu which affords a psychosocial climate geared to the reduction of dependency upon alcohol. The ultimate goal of such a residential rehabilitation setting is the return of the client to the community, with an increased capability to function independently and with the ability to function without or with much less dependency upon alcohol.

Such a residential setting is a type of "halfway house." The use of halfway houses as rehabilitation facilities for alcohol dependents is not new. However, the residential treatment setting recommended here would consist of far more than the conventional residence for alcohol addicts. It would be a carefully planned multi-stage system of transitional rehabilitation, based on specific social and psychological principles. If we are to be guided by the findings of this study, then such a residential setting must embody the following basic principles of operation:

1. All activities in the treatment setting would be designed to fulfill the function of replacement of family loss. Referring to the finding of replicated loss for many of the subjects, it becomes more evident that the alcohol dependent has sustained a heavy toll in emotional loss of family members. Thus, his normal dependency patterns have been interrupted and sharply curtailed. In order to enable him to relinquish his drinking patterns, the residential setting must provide a group of family relationships within which he can initially express and later understand and work through his dependent strivings.

In this context, staff must be able to offer strong parental relationships to the alcohol dependent client while other resident patients function in sibling roles. The strong need for a family setting cannot be overemphasized. The family atmosphere would allow the alcohol dependent a target for his massive initial dependency as well as provide close relationships which can later serve to motivate the client to abandon his drinking habits and take up a life style which falls within the normative framework of society.

2. A second basic principle of operation would be the bidirectional transitional movement of clients. To move clients from the highly sheltered dependent milieu of the halfway house directly into community life frequently results in their being overwhelmed by the immediacy of demands for independent functioning. This is supported by the findings that indicate, for many, a poor capacity for negotiating within social systems as a consequence of lack of early experience in social skills development. Therefore, a series of steps or stages would be designed to ease the alcohol dependent client back into community life.

The detailed operating process of such a facility will be explained below. However, a major advantage of the facility being proposed is that the transition to community living is not unidirectional or irreversible, but rather bidirectional. In other words, if the alcohol dependent is failing to negotiate successfully through a particular stage of independent functioning, he is moved back to a previous stage and worked with until his *motivational level exceeds his dependency strivings* and he is ready to attempt to move again toward the next stage of independence.

3. The third principle which would guide this residential rehabilitation facility is intensive thrust motivation. In other words, every staff member, as well as the more independent patient members of the facility, would persist in constant efforts to evoke independent action from the alcohol dependent. The motivational process would involve using the strength of close interpersonal relationships to help the client achieve the insight that the rewards of normative participation in society are worth the stresses sustained in independently coping with the psychosocial buffetings of life.

The residential treatment facility for alcohol dependent clients would be modeled, with some modifications, after a program of rehabilitation of chronic psychotic patients called the "Member Employee Program," developed by Peffer, Margolin, Stotsky and Mason (1957). This program was uniquely successful in that in seven years it rehabilitated from a fifty-bed dormitory of one hospital eight hundred of the most difficult patients, many of whom were considered hopeless. Some of these patients were alcohol dependents able to reduce their drinking to the point of making adequate social and vocational adjustments. The program was based on the movement of patients through a series of transitional phases, each involving greater independence, with intensive supportive counseling throughout each phase.

1. The first phase of the transitional residential system would be similar to a hospital in its psychsocial climate. In this phase many of the alcohol dependent's infantile dependency needs would be gratified during a period of intensive care. When joint staff decision considered the client ready, staff members would begin to prepare the alcohol dependent for the second phase by using their relationship with the patient to motivate him to attempt a higher level of independent functioning. As part of this phase, the client is helped to move into various rehabilitation activities (such as occupational therapy etc.) dependent upon his needs.
2. In the second phase the client would be moved into a special dormitory on the grounds with other clients at approximately the same stage of development. However, the general psychosocial climate would differ greatly from that of the hospital. In the first phase most of the client's needs were met by staff in a way which accepted dependence. In the dormitory phase, clients would do things for themselves and govern themselves. Active attempts would be made by staff and the hospital organizational structure to decrease the client's dependency. He would be discharged officially from the hospital, given the new status of "employee," and hired for remunerative employment on jobs existing in the organizational structure of the institution. If, in this intrainstitutional employment, the client shows satisfactory vocational adjustment (i.e., work performance, relationship to superiors, and functioning in work groups) he would be advanced to the third phase.
3. In the third phase, the alcohol dependent would be placed in a regular job outside the institution's grounds but would still live temporarily in the dormitory. Again his social and vocational adjustment in terms of "work satisfaction" and "satisfactoriness" (Lofquist, 1964) would be carefully observed. When his capacity for maintaining social and emotional relationships was judged to be adequate, the client would be advanced to the final phase.
4. In the final phase the client would be moved out of the dormitory and begin to assume roles of full community living. Supportive

counseling would decrease in intensity as the client demonstrated the capacity for a good psychosocial and vocational adjustment with highly reduced or no dependence upon alcohol. With some clients, minimal, infrequent, supportive counseling would have to continue indefinitely to provide security in the knowledge that the counselor is there to help if he is needed.

In all four phases of the residential program, the role of the counselor would be crucial:

1. Above all, the counselor must be highly supportive so that the client feels secure in knowing he would be accepted by and could count on the counselor, no matter what.
2. The counselor must be directive and, in many instances, forceful in guiding and reassuring the client.
3. The rehabilitation counselor must communicate with the client in language and symbol emotionally meaningful to the particular patient. For example, if profanity is effective, profanity should be used.
4. The client must be prepared emotionally for each succeeding phase by the counselor through extensive discussion as well as through various group-dynamics techniques such as role playing etc. For example, if the client is being prepared for a job interview, the situation can be role played. Even though the counselor should make it clear that he will not accept unacceptable behavior, his acceptance of the patient as a personality with value and integrity must never wane.
5. It is imperative that the client be carefully followed up in the community and always aware that, if needed, he can count on the support of the rehabilitation counselor. The counselor, on the other hand, would maintain an attitudinal structure within which he was not disappointed, abashed, or overconcerned with any alcohol dependent behavior or episodes into which the client might lapse. The alcohol dependent behavior would not be dwelled upon or accentuated. Instead, the normative elements of the client's behavior should be stressed and built upon.
6. Crucial to the process is the client's knowledge that if he fails, the counselor would not berate him, think less of him, or give up on him. He should be made strongly aware of the counselor's faith in his ultimate success. Current failure should mean return to an earlier phase of the program and the opportunity to try again. In other words, current failure should not mean permanent failure.

The findings of this study lend particular emphasis to the importance of role models for masculine identification. Since a sizable minority of the alcohol dependents came from a home in which either the mother was dominant (decision maker) or the father was absent the opportunity to establish an adequate masculine identity must be presented. If the alcohol dependent is in outpatient rehabilitation counseling, then the counselor must provide this model. If the alcohol dependent is being treated in a transitional residential system then a central significant figure (Stotsky et al., 1958) must act as a role model.

The findings also suggest the value of involving women in the treatment of the male alcohol dependent, both as counselors and as inpatient staff in residential rehabilitation treatment institutions. Since some of the alcohol dependents had experienced a relationship with a dominant and/or overprotective mother, and many reported not getting along with their spouses, their relationships with women may have been inadequate. Thus, exposure to female rehabilitation counselors as well as female residential treatment staff, women who are warm, feminine, accepting and noncontrolling, affords the alcohol dependent an opportunity for a reeducational experience. We might even suggest the creation of residential rehabilitation centers for the alcohol dependent which would be "coeducational." This type of facility would enable certain clients whose problem is related to an inability to form adequate heterosexual relationships to do so in an atmosphere that is controlled and supportive.

When rehabilitation of the alcohol dependent takes place, either inpatient or outpatient, providing the client with opportunities for the development of social skills is crucial. Group-dynamics techniques, group counseling, group recreation, and productive activities should be stressed along with group exercises designed to reestablish social identity. Through role playing and other techniques, the alcohol dependent client should be given ample opportunity for actual practice in social relationships.

Reachout or aggressive casework techniques in the rehabilitation of the alcohol dependent should be stressed. It should be remembered that the application, the request, or the reaching out for treatment is essentially a social negotiation. It involves a certain amount of social confrontation of a social institution, a process of which many alcohol dependents are emotionally incapable. They may be quickly frightened and "turned off' by the bureaucratic red tape involved in intake procedures. Consequently, it becomes necessary that the treatment facility offer services aggressively and takes responsibility for the psychosocial transactions relevant to the setting up of treatment. Since 42 percent of the alcohol dependents in this study reported some chronic physical ailment, the rehabilitation of the actual physical condition of the client is a good starting point and may result in the client's involvement in rehabilitation for his dependence upon alcohol.

In conclusion, the rehabilitation potential of these skid-row alcohol dependents can be viewed with guarded optimism. Too long and too frequently professionals charged with their rehabilitation have looked upon them with pessimism; a pessimism which was nonverbally communicated to the client and contributed to his low motivation. The subjects who participated in this study had truly skidded to the proverbial bottom of the heap. Yet, they still showed the desire to relate to the interviewers and gained gratification from the interview itself. Moreover, their biographies indicated periods in their lives when they were engaged in meaningful and productive activity.

Finally, some of the alcohol dependents in this study could be described as "aggressive dependent" (Usdane, personal communication). That is to say, these men often engaged in a remarkable amount of independent behavior in order to remain dependent. Paradoxical as this may seem, it is nonetheless true. The life style of the skid-row alcohol dependent, as observed by this research team, while dependent in terms of the norms and values of society, required much in the way of initiative and independent functioning if he was to meet his concrete needs in the skid-row "jungle" habitat.

Finding a place to sleep at night becomes a major problem in this "Bowery" type of existence. Some could obtain shelter and a bed when they were fortunate enough to be able to scrape up fifty cents; others, not in possession of fifty cents, as was frequently the case, walked the streets all night or sought the shelter of an unfrequented doorway or vacant automobile. Competition for earning opportunities, food, and the maintenance of an adequate supply of alcohol required much ingenuity. To survive in this milieu necessitates a high degree of independent behavior. By the standards of society it is a pathological type of independent behavior. Approaching the problem from this point of view, we cannot help but speculate on the rehabilitation potential of these men, if their pathologically independent behavior could be diverted into socially acceptable channels.

The authors by no means profess to have the key to the successful rehabilitation of the alcohol dependent. Yet, we do believe that, within a rehabilitation setting that offers the alcohol dependent acceptance of his dependency, he can be retrained in the social negotiative skills. Once he gains the security born of adequate social experience and success in psychosocial transactions, he may no longer need the chemical support of liquor. Gratification, hopefully, will come from people, not from the bottle.

References

References

Allen, L. R., & Dootjes, I. Some personality considerations of an alcoholic population. *Perceptual and Motor Skills,* 1968, **27**(3), 707-712.

Anderson, N. The hobo. Chicago: University of Chicago Press, 1923.

Androes, L., McKenzie, L., & Chotlos, J. The "game" and alcoholic patients. *American Journal of Nursing,* 1967 **67**(8), 1672-1674.

Armstrong, R. G. A review of the theories explaining the psychodynamics and etiology of alcoholism in men. *Psychology Newsletter,* 1959, **10**, 159-171.

Bacon, S. D. Inebriety, social integration, and marriage. *Quarterly Journal of Studies on Alcohol,* 1944, **5**, 86-125, 303-339.

Bacon, S. D., & Roth, F. L. Drunkeness in wartime Connecticut. Paper. Hartford: Connecticut War Council, 1943.

Bahr, H. M. Drinking interaction and identification: notes on socialization into skid row. *Journal of Health and Social Behavior,* 1967, **8**(4), 272-285.

Bahr, H. M., & Langfer, S. J. Social attachment and drinking in skid-row life histories. *Social Problems,* 1967, **14**, 464-472.

Bailey, M. B. Alcoholism and marriage. A review of research and professional literature. *Quarterly Journal of Studies on Alcohol,* 1961, **22**, 81-97.

Baken, D. The relationship between alcoholism and birth rank. *Quarterly Journal of Studies on Alcohol,* 1949, **10**, 434-440.

Barrett, T. M. Chronic alcoholism in veterans. *Quarterly Journal of Studies pn Alcohol,* 1943, **4**, 68-78.

Barton, W. E. Deficits in the treatment of alcoholism and recommendations for correction. *American Journal of Psychiatry,* 1968, **124**(12), 1679-1686.

Bell, R. G. Defensive thinking in alcohol addicts. *Canadian Medical Association Journal,* 1965, **92**, 228.

Blum, E. M. Psychoanalytic views of alcoholism. *Quarterly Journal of Studies on Alcohol,* 1966, **27**, 259-299.

Blumberg, L., Shipley, T. E., Jr., Shandler, I. W., & Neibuhr, H. The development, major goals and strategies of a skid row program: Philadelphia. *Quarterly Journal of Studies on Alcohol,* 1966, **27**, 244.

Blume, S. B., & Shepard, C. The changing effects of drinking on the changing personalities of alcoholics. *Quarterly Journal of Studies on Alcohol,* 1967, **28**(3), 436-443.

Brotman, R., & Freedman, A. M. Intervention targets in the community mental health rehabilitation of alcohol users. *American Journal of Orthopsychiatry*, 1967, 37(2), 280-281.

Button, A. D. The genesis and development of alcoholism: An empirically based schema. *Quarterly Journal of Studies on Alcohol,* 1956, 17, 671-675.

Canter, F. Personality factors related to participation in treatment by hospitalized male alcoholics. *Journal of Clinical Psychology,* 1966, 22(1), 114-116.

Caplan, G. *An approach to community mental health.* Grune, 1961.

Chafetz, M. E. Research in the alcohol clinic and around-the-clock psychiatric service of the Massachusetts General Hospital. *American Journal of Psychiatry,* 1968, 124(12), 1674-1679.

Chafetz, M. E., Demone, H. W., Jr., & Solomon, H. C. Alcoholism: its cause and prevention. *New York Journal of Medicine,* 1962, 62, 1614-1625.

Chodorkoff, B. Alcoholism and ego function. *Quarterly Journal of Studies on Alcohol,* 1964, 25, 292-299.

Clifford, B. J. A study of the wives of rehabilitated and unrehabilitated alcoholics. *Social Casework,* 1960, 41, 457-460.

Conger, J. J. Reinforcement theory and the dynamics of alcoholism. *Quarterly Journal of Studies on Alcohol, 1956,* 17, 296-305.

Couch, A. S. Data-Text System: A Computer Language for Social Science Research. Preliminary Manual, 1967.

Crabtree, F. E. Alcoholism: A social psychological study. *Dissertation Abstracts,* 1966, 26, 2606-6207.

Crowne, D. P., & Marlowe, D. *The approval motive: studies in evaluative dependence.* New York: Wiley, 1964.

Dabrowski, K. *Positive disintegration.* Boston: Little, Brown, 1964. p. 132.

DeLint, J. E. E. Alcoholism, birth rank and parental deprivation. *American Journal of Psychiatry,* 1964, 120, 1062-1065.

deSaugy, D. The alcoholic and his wife: a psychosocial and statistical study of the conditions of their individual development and their life together. *L'Hygiene mentale,* 1962, 51, 145-201.

Devrient, P., & Lolli, G. Choice of alcoholic beverages among 240 alcoholics in Switzerland, *Quarterly Journal of Studies on Alcohol,* 1962, 23, 459-467.

Dollard, J., & Miller, N. E. *Personality and psychotherapy.* New York: McGraw-Hill, 1950.

Falkey, D. B., & Scheyer, S. Characteristics of male alcoholics admitted to the medical ward of a general hospital. *Quarterly Journal of Studies on Alcohol,* 1957, **18**, 67-97.

Feeney, F. E., Mindlin, D. F., Minear, V. H., & Short, E. E. The challenge of the skid row alcoholic. *Quarterly Journal of Studies on Alcohol,* 1955, **16**, 645-667.

Fenichel, O. *The psychoanalytic theory of neurosis.* New York: Norton, 1945. Pp. 375-380.

Ferneau, E. W., Jr., Individual therapy with the alcoholic patient. *Diseases of the Nervous System,* 1968, **29**(10), 684-687.

Floch, M. Imprisoned abnormal drinkers: application of the Bowman-Jellinek classification schedule to an institutional sample. Part I. Review and analysis of data. *Quarterly Journal of Studies on Alcohol,* 1947, **7**, 518-566.

Fowler, R. D., Jr., Teel, S. K., & Coyle, F. A., Jr. The measurement of alcoholic response to treatment by Barron's ego-strength scale. *Journal of Psychology,* 1967, **67**(1), 65-68.

Fox, R. Psychiatric aspects of alcoholism. *American Journal of Psychotherapy,* 1965, **19**, 408-416.

Fox, V., & Lowe, G. D. Day-hospital treatment of the alcoholic patient. *Quarterly Journal of Studies on Alcohol,* 1968, **29**, 634-641.

Franks, C. M. Alcohol, alcoholism, and conditioning. A review of the literature and some theoretical considerations. *Journal of Mental Science,* 1958, **104**, 14-33.

Gerard, D. L., Saenger, G., & Wile, R. The abstinent alcoholic. *A.M.A. Archives of General Psychiatry,* 1962, **6**, 83-95.

Goldin, G., & Perry, S. Dependency and its implications for rehabilitation. *Northeastern Studies in Vocational Rehabilitation, Monogr. 1,* April, 1967.

Grosz, H. J. Birth order, anxiety, and affiliative tendency. Observations and comments regarding Schachter's hypothesis. *Journal of Nervous and Mental Disease,* 1964, **139**(6), 588-590.

Heilizer, F. Conflict models, alcohol, and drinking patterns. *Journal of Psychology,* 1964, **57**, 457-473.

Hershenson, D. B. Stress induced use of alcohol by problem drinkers as a function of their sense of identity. *Quarterly Journal of Studies on Alcohol,* 1965, **26**, 213-222.

Higgins, J. W. Psychodynamics in the excessive drinking of alcohol. *A.M.A. Archives of Neurology and Psychiatry,* 1953, **69**, 713-727.

Hilgard, J. R., & Newman, M. F. Parental loss by death in childhood as an etiological factor among schizophrenic and alcoholic patients compared with a non-patient community sample. *Journal of Nervous and Mental Disease,* 1963, **137**, 14-28.

Hochwald, H. L. The occupational performance of thirty alcoholic men. *Quarterly Journal of Studies on Alcohol,* 1951, **12**, 612-620.

Hurwitz, J. I., & Lelos, D. A. A multilevel interpersonal profile of employed alcoholics. *Quarterly Journal of Studies on Alcohol,* 1968, 29(1-A), 64-76.

Jackson, J. K., & Connor, R. Attitudes of the parents of alcoholics, moderate drinkers, and non-drinkers toward drinking. *Quarterly Journal of Studies on Alcohol,* 1953, 14, 596-613.

Jones, M. C. Personality correlates and antecedents of drinking patterns in adult males. *Journal of Consulting and Clinical Psychology,* 1968, 32(1), 2-12.

Katz, L. The salvation army men's social center: II results. *Quarterly Journal of Studies on Alcohol,* 1966, 27(4), 636-647.

Kaufman, I., & Heims, L. The body image of the juvenile delinquent. *American Journal of Orthopsychiatry,* 1958, **28**, 146-159.

Kepner, E. Application of learning theory to the etiology and treatment of alcoholism. *Quarterly Journal of Studies on Alcohol,* 1964, **25**, 279-291.

Kingham, R. J. Alcoholism and the reinforcement theory of learning. *Quarterly Journal of Studies on Alcohol,* 1958, **19**, 320-330.

Knight, R. P. The psychodynamics of chronic alcoholism. *Journal of Nervous and Mental Disease,* 1937, **86**, 538-548.

Laubach, F. C. *Why there are vagrants.* New York: 1916.

Lemert, E. M. Dependency in married alcoholics. *Quarterly Journal of Studies on Alcohol,* 1962, **23**(4), 590-609.

Levy, R. I. The psychodynamic functions of alcohol. *Quarterly Journal of Studies on Alcohol,* 1958, **19**, 649-659.

Liansky, E. S. The etiology of alcoholism: the role of psychological predisposition. *Quarterly Journal of Studies on Alcohol,* 1960, **21**, 314.

Lindemann, E., Chafetz, M. E., & Blane, H. T. Alcohol crisis treatment approach and establishment of treatment relations with alcoholics. *Psychological Reports,* 1963, **12**, 862.

Lindt, H. The rescue fantasy in group treatment of alcoholics. *International Journal of Group Psychotherapy,* 1959, **9**, 43-52.

Locke, B. Z. Outcome of first hospitalization of patients with alcoholic psychoses. *Quarterly Journal of Studies on Alcohol,* 1962, **23**, 640-643.

Lofquist, L. H. Disability and work. *Minnesota Studies in Vocational Rehabilitation*, 1964, No. 17.

Lolli, G., Golder, G., Serianni, E., Bonfiglio, G., & Balboni, C. Choice of alcoholic beverage among 178 alcoholics in Italy. *Quarterly Journal of Studies on Alcohol*, 1958, 19, 303-315.

Lolli, G., Schesler, E., & Golder, G. Choice of alcoholic beverage among 105 alcoholics in New York. *Quarterly Journal of Studies on Alcohol*, 1960, 21, 475-482.

Malzberg, B. A study of first admissions with alcoholic psychoses in New York State. *Quarterly Journal of Studies on Alcohol*, 1947, 8, 274-295.

Malzberg, B. First admissions with alcoholic psychoses in New York State, year ended March 31, 1948. With note on first admissions for alcoholism without psychoses. *Quarterly Journal of Studies on Alcohol*, 1949, 11, 461-470.

Margolin, R. J. Member employee program: new hope for the mentally ill. *American Archives of Rehabilitation Therapy*, 1955, 3, 69-81.

Markham, J. E. Sociological aspects of alcohol and food deviations. *Annals of the New York Academy of Sciences*, 1966, 133(3), 814-819.

Martensen-Larsen, O. The family constellation analysis and male alcoholism. *Acta Genetics*, 1957, 7, 441-444.

Maslow, A. H. *Motivation and personality*, New York: Harper & Brothers, 1954.

Maxwell, M. A., Lemere, F., & O'Hollaren, P. Changing characteristics of private-hospital alcoholic patients — a 20 year time-trend analysis. *Quarterly Journal of Studies on Alcohol*, 1958, 19, 309-319.

Mayer, J., Needham, M. A., & Myerson, D. J. Contact and initial attendance at an alcoholism clinic. *Quarterly Journal of Studies on Alcohol*, 1965, 26, 480-485.

McCord, W., McCord, J., & Gudeman, J. Some current theories of alcoholism: a longitudinal evaluation. *Quarterly Journal of Studies on Alcohol*, 1959, 20, 727-749.

McCullough, W. E. A two-year survey of alcoholic patients in a California state hospital, *Quarterly Journal of Studies on Alcohol*, 1952, 13, 240-253.

Meyerson, D. J. An active therapeutic method of interrupting the dependency relationship of certain male alcoholics. *Quarterly Journal of Studies on Alcohol*, 1953, 14, 419-426.

Moon, L. E., & Patton, R. E. Alcoholic psychotic in the New York

State Mental Hospitals. *Quarterly Journal of Studies on Alcohol,* 1963, 24, 664-681.

Moore, R. A., & Murphy, T. C. Denial of alcoholism as an obstacle to recovery. *Quarterly Journal of Studies on Alcohol,* 1961, 22, 597-609.

Moore, R. A., & Ramseur, F. A study of the background of 100 hospitalized veterans with alcoholism. *Quarterly Journal of Studies on Alcohol,* 1960, 21, 51-67.

Munt, J. S. Fear of dependency: a factor in casework with alcoholics. *Social Work,* 1960, 5(1), 27-32.

Navran, L. A rationally derived MMPI scale to measure dependence. *Journal of Consulting Psychology,* 1954, 18, 192.

Navratil, L. On the etiology of alcoholism. *Quarterly Journal of Studies on Alcohol,* 1959, 20, 236-244.

Navratil, L., & Wein, Z. The role of the wife in the pathogenesis of alcoholism. *Nerveneilk,* 1957, 14, 90-97.

Newell, N. Alcoholism and the father-image. *Quarterly Journal of Studies on Alcohol,* 1950, 11, 92-96.

Oltman, J. E., & Friedman, S. A. A consideration of parental deprivation and other factors in alcohol addicts. *Quarterly Journal of Studies on Alcohol,* 1953, 14, 49-57.

Oltman, J. E., McGarry, J. J., & Friedman, S. Parental deprivation and the "broken home" in dementia praecox and other mental disorders. *American Journal of Psychiatry,* 1952, 108, 685-693.

Partington, J. T., & Johnson, F. G. Personality types among alcoholics. *Quarterly Journal of Studies on Alcohol,* 1969, 30(1-A), 21-34.

Pattison, E. M. A critique of alcoholism treatment concepts. *Quarterly Journal of Studies on Alcohol,* 1966, 27, 49-71.

Pattison, E. M., Coe, R., & Rhodes, R. J. Evaluation of alcoholism treatment: a comparison of three facilities. *Archives of General Psychiatry,* 1969, 20(4), 478-488.

Peffer, P. A., Margolin, R. J., Stotsky, B. A., & Mason, A. S. (Eds.) *Member employee program: a new approach to the rehabilitation of the chronic mental patient.* Brockton, Mass.: V.A. Hospital, 1957.

Pittman, D. J., & Gordon, C. W. Revolving door: a study of the chronic police case inebriate. *Monographs of the Yale Center of Alcohol Studies,* New Haven: Free Press, 1958. No. 2.

Pittman, D. J., & Snyder, C. R. *Society, culture, and drinking patterns.* New York: Wiley, 1962.

Prout, C. T., Strongin, E. I., & White, M. A. A study of results in hospital treatment of alcoholism in males. *American Journal of Psychiatry,* 1950, **107,** 14-19.

Rado, S. Psychoanalysis of pharmacothymia. *Psychoanalytic Quarterly,* 1933, **2,** 1-23.

Rathod, N. H., Gregory, E., Blows, D., & Thomas, G. H. A two year followup study of alcoholic patients. *British Journal of Psychiatry,* 1966, **112,** 683-692.

Reader, D. H. Alcoholism and excessive drinking: a sociological review. *Psychologia Africana, Monograph Supplement* (No. 3), 1967, p. 69.

Rooney, J. F. Group processes among skid row winos — a reevaluation of the undersocialization hypothesis. *Quarterly Journal of Studies on Alcohol,* 1961, **22**(3), 444-460.

Rossi, J. J., Stach, A., & Bradley, J. Effects of treatment of male alcoholics in a mental hospital. A follow-up study. *Quarterly Journal of Studies on Alcohol,* 1963, **24,** 91-108.

Rudd, J. L., & Margolin, R. J. Educational Therapy: past, present, and future. *Rehabilitation Literature,* 1970, **31**(4), 98-102.

Sadoun, R., & Lolli, G. Choice of alcoholic beverage among 120 alcoholics in France. *Quarterly Journal of Studies on Alcohol,* 1962, **23,** 449-458.

Schachter, S. *The psychology of affiliation.* Stanford: Stanford University Press, 1959.

Schafer, R. Regression in the service of the ego: the relevance of a psychoanalytic concept for personality assessment. In Gardner Lindzey (Ed.), *Assessment of human motives.* New York: Grove Press, 1960.

Schwaab, E. Dependency factors in relation to recall of dependency material. *Dissertation Abstracts,* 1959, **20,** 1441-1442.

Selzer, M., & Holloway, W. A follow-up of alcoholics committed to a state hospital. *Quarterly Journal of Studies on Alcohol,* 1957, **18,** 97-120.

Shaw, I. A. The treatment of alcoholism with tetraethylthiuram disulfate in a state mental hospital. *Quarterly Journal of Studies on Alcohol,* 1951, **12,** 576-577 (577).

Singer, E., Blane, H. T., & Kasschau, R. Alcoholism and social isolation. *Journal of Abnormal and Social Psychology,* 1964, **69**(6), 681-685.

Smart, R. G. Alcoholism, birth order and family size. *Journal of Abnormal and Social Psychology,* 1963, **66,** 17-23.

Smith, C. M. Family size in alcoholism. *Journal of Abnormal and Social Psychology,* 1965, **70,** 230.

Smith, C. M., & McIntyre, S. Family size, birth rank, and ordinal position in psychiatric illness. *Canadian Psychiatric Association Journal*, 1963, **8**, 244-248.

Solenberger, A. W. *One thousand homeless men.* New York: Charities Publication Committee, 1911.

Sterne, M. W., & Pittman, D. J. The concept of motivation: A source of institutional and professional blockage in the treatment of alcoholics. *Quarterly Journal of Studies on Alcohol*, 1965, **26**, 41-57.

Storm, T., & Smart, R. G. Dissociation: a possible explanation of some features of alcoholism nd implications for its treatment. *Quarterly Journal of Studies on Alcohol*, 1965, **26**, 111-115.

Stotsky, B. A., Mason, A. S., & Samaras, M. Significant figures in the rehabilitation of chronic mental patients. *Journal of Chronic Diseases*, 1958, **7**(2), 131-139.

Straus, R. Alcohol and the homeless man. *Quarterly Journal of Studies on Alcohol*, 1946, **7**, 360-404.

Straus, R., & Bacon, S. D. Alcoholism and social stability. A study of occupational integration in 2023 male clinic patients. *Quarterly Journal of Studies on Alcohol*, 1951, **12**, 231-260.

Straus, R., & McCarthy, R. G. Nonaddictive pathological drinking patterns of homeless men. *Quarterly Journal of Studies on Alcohol*, 1951, **12**, 601-611.

Sutherland, E. H., & Locke, H. J. *Twenty thousand homeless men.* Chicago: University of Chicago Press, 1936.

Swensen, C. H., Jr., & Davis, H. C. Types of workhouse inmate alcoholics. *Quarterly Journal of Studies on Alcohol, 1959*, **20**, 757-766.

Tahka, V. The alcoholic personality. *The Finnish Foundation for Alcohol Studies*, Helsinki: Finland, 1966.

Terry, J., Lolli, G., & Golder, G. Choice of alcoholic beverage among 531 alcoholics in California. *Quarterly Journal of Studies on Alcohol*, 1957, **18**, 417-428.

Thomas, R. E., Gliedman, L. H., Freund, J., Imber, S. D., & Stone, A. R. Favorable response in the clinical treatment of chronic alcoholism. *Journal of the American Medical Association*, 1959, **169**, 1994-1997.

Trice, H. M. *Alcoholism in America.* New York: McGraw-Hill, 1966.

Trice, H. M. Alcoholism: Group factors in etiology and therapy. *Human Organization*, 1956, **15**(2), 33-40.

Trice, H. M., & Pittman, D. J. Social organization and alcoholism:

A review of significant research since 1940. *Social Problems,* 1958, 5(4), 294-307.

Ullman, A. D. The first drinking experience of "addictive" and "normal" drinkers. *Quarterly Journal of Studies on Alcohol,* 1953, 14, 181-191.

Usdane, W. Personal Communication with R. J. Margolin.

Vogel-Sprott, M. D. *Birth order and personality characteristics of alcoholics.* Toronto, Ont., 1963, Mimeo.

Wahl, C. W. Some antecedent factors in the family histories of 109 alcoholics. *Quarterly Journal of Studies on Alcohol,* 1956, 17, 643-654.

Walcott, E. P., & Straus, R. Use of a hospital facility in conjunction with outpatient clinics in the treatment of alcoholics. *Quarterly Journal of Studies on Alcohol,* 1952, 13, 60-77.

Wallerstein, R. S., et. al. *Hospital treatment of alcoholism: a comparative experimental study.* New York: Basic Books, 1957.

Weiss, D., & Margolin, R. J. A re-evaluation of educational therapy for psychotic patients. In J. L. Rudd and R. J. Margolin (Eds.), *Selected Readings in Rehabilitation.* Medford, Mass.: R.M.D. Publishers, 1969.

Wellman, W. M., Maxwell, M. A., & O'Hollaren, P. Private hospital alcoholic patients and the changing conception of the "typical" alcoholic. *Quarterly Journal of Studies on Alcohol,* 1957, 18, 388-404.

Wenger, P. History of a drinking habit in 400 inmates of a penal institution. *New York State Journal of Medicine,* 1944, 44, 1898-1904.

Wetherbee, M. E. Conflict resolution in two types of alcoholics. *Dissertation Abstracts,* 1966, 27(5-B), 1632-1633.

White, W. F., & Porter, T. L. Self-concept reports among hospitalized alcoholics during early periods of sobriety. *Journal of Consulting Psychology,* 1966, 13(3), 352-355.

Wilbur, B. M., Salkin, D., & Birnbaum, H. The response of tuberculous alcoholics to a therapeutic community. *Quarterly Journal of Studies on Alcohol,* 1966, 27, 620-635.

Williams, J. H. Vocational rehabilitation of treated alcoholics. *State of Florida Alcoholic Rehabilitation Program,* Avon Park, 1964.

Williams, J. H. Follow-up adjustment of alcoholic referrals for vocational rehabilitation. *State of Florida Alcoholic Rehabilitation Program,* Avon Park, 1967.

Wolf, I. Alcoholism and marriage. *Quarterly Journal of Studies on Alcohol,* 1958, 19, 511-513.

World Health Organization. Expert committee on mental health, alcoholism sub-committee 2nd report. Report, 1952, No. 48.

Zax, M., Marsey, R., & Biggs, C. Demographic characteristics of alcoholic outpatients and the tendency to remain in treatment. *Quarterly Journal of Studies on Alcohol,* 1961, **22,** 98-105.

About the Authors

Bernard Stotsky is an M.D. whose past affiliations included Director of Psychological Services, Veterans Administration Hospital, Brockton; faculty of Boston University and Duke University Medical School. Currently a practicing psychiatrist, he is a research consultant to New England Rehabilitation Research Institute. He has published several books on geriatric psychiatry and has published widely in the field of rehabilitation, psychology, and medicine.

Sally Perry is a research associate at the New England Rehabilitation Research Institute. She received her B.S. and M.S. in psychology from the University of Massachusetts and has participated in a number of research studies in the areas of motivation and dependency.

George J. Goldin is director of research at the New England Rehabilitation Research Institute and professor of special education at Northeastern University, Boston, Massachusetts. He received his B.S. degree in psychology from the University of Massachusetts, his M.S. in psychiatric social work from Boston University, and his Ph.D. degree from Brandeis University. He has had extensive experience in the fields of mental health, family counseling, community planning and social welfare. His background includes positions on clinical practice, supervisory, administrative and planning levels. He is the author of numerous articles and monographs in the field of rehabilitation, the sociology of organizations and various phases of social work.

Reuben J. Margolin is currently Chairman of the Department of Rehabilitation and Special Education and Project Director of the New England Regional Rehabilitation Research Institute which is funded by the Rehabilitation Services Administration. The Institute has as its core area the relationship of motivation to dependency in the rehabilitation of the disabled.

Prior to coming to Northeastern University, he was counseling psychologist and Director of the Member Employee Rehabilitation Work Program at the Veterans Administration Hospital in Brockton.

He is rehabilitation consultant to many agencies, including Veterans Administration, World University in Puerto Rico, Massachusetts Department of Mental Health, and Morgan Memorial. He has received outstanding achievement awards from the President's Committee on Employing the Handicapped, American Association of

Medical Rehabilitation Directors and Coordinators, Massachusetts Federation of Nursing Homes, and the National Conference of Christians and Jews.

He has published five books and over 100 articles.